Submitted

40 FEATURE

Behind the Story
Real-life stories of true humility. *by Hayley DiMarco*

43 POP QUIZ

How humble are YOU?

44 DEEPER

Not About Me: The Humility of Surrender
Find out why humility is an important part of surrender. *by Hayley DiMarco*

48 FEATURE

A Humble Heart
One teen's tale of following God's call. *by Missy Faulkenberry*

49 VOICES

What in your life do you need wisdom about?

50 FEATURE

What Happens When . . .
A guide to making wise decisions? *by Kelly King*

54 ASK HAYLEY

55 7 DAYS

7 ways you can practice humility.

RELEASED

58 FEATURE

Oh, the Guilt!
The difference between good and bad guilt— and why neither has to rule your life. *by Hayley DiMarco*

61 POP QUIZ

Where's your focus?

62 DEEPER

Released: The Brokenness of Surrender
The story of Rahab tells us God makes broken lives beautiful. *by Hayley DiMarco*

66 FEATURE

Restored
Meet a living example of God's power to redeem. *by Hannah Wakefield*

67 VOICES

What do you wish you'd never done?

68 FEATURE

Three Days that Changed My Life
One woman's story of abandonment, rescue, and, ultimately, forgiveness. *by Dawn Cornelius*

72 ASK HAYLEY

73 7 DAYS

7 ways you can let go of your past.

Sacrificed

76 FEATURE

*Friends Forever: How To Be
a Good Friend*
Discover six characteristics of a godly friend.
by Hayley DiMarco

79 POP QUIZ

What kind of friend are you?

80 DEEPER

Love Is a Verb: Sacrificial Love and Surrender
Dig deeper into the concept of sacrificial love by
studying Ruth's story. *by Hayley DiMarco*

84 FEATURE

Devoted
Elizabeth and Rachel share what devotion
really looks like. *by Hannah Wakefield*

85 VOICES

When has a friend sacrificed something for you?

86 FEATURE

Toxic Friendships: Are You Safe?
How to tell if you're in a toxic friendship.
by Emily Cole

90 ASK HAYLEY

91 7 DAYS

7 ways to love sacrificially.

Compelled

94 FEATURE

The Power of Prayer
Check out these real-life stories of the power
of prayer. *by Hayley DiMarco*

97 POP QUIZ

What's your prayer personality?

98 DEEPER

*Do Something:
Compelled to Action*
Dig into Scripture to study Esther's story—
and how surrender is a call to action.
by Hayley DiMarco

102 FEATURE

Courageous
Skyler is committed to sharing her faith with her
friends, even if she can't see what He's doing.
by Hannah Wakefield

103 VOICES

When have *you* had to take a stand?

104 FEATURE

For Such a Time as This
You don't need to be a "better" Christian.
You need to be a believer who is surrendered
to God. *by Amy Pierson*

108 ASK HAYLEY

109 7 DAYS

7 ways you can intercede.

committed

112 FEATURE

The Ripple Effect: Living a Legacy
God can use your surrender to create a legacy.
by Hayley DiMarco

115 POP QUIZ

Worrier or Warrior?

116 DEEPER

Make a Commitment: The Sweet Safety of Surrender
The life of surrender is one of deep commitment. *by Hayley DiMarco*

120 FEATURE

Alma's Legacy
Without Alma's commitment to Christ, Hannah's life would look very different. *by Hannah Wakefield*

121 VOICES

Who has changed your life?

122 FEATURE

Kyla's Choice: Part 2
Choose the ending to Kyla's story. *by Emily White*

126 ASK HAYLEY

127 7 DAYS

7 ways you can leave a legacy.

128 LAST WORDS

SIMPLE SURRENDER

Team Leader **Mike Wakefield**
Content Editor **Mandy Crow**
Production Editor **Scott Latta**
Graphic Designer **Amy Lyon**

Writer **Hayley DiMarco**

Contributing Writers **Emily White, Hannah Wakefield, Julie Fidler, Jennifer Grether, Katie Headley, Kelly King, Dawn Cornelius, Emily Cole, Amy Pierson, and Missy Faulkenberry, courtesty of** *essential connection.*

Simple Surrender (ISBN: 9781415877760 Item Number: 005558674) Dewey Decimal Classification Number: 248.83 Subject Heading: GIRLS \ CHRISTIAN LIFE \ PROVIDENCE AND GOVERNMENT OF GOD Published by LifeWay Press® Copyright © 2012 No part of this work may be reproduced or transmitted in any form or by any means, electronic or mechanical, including photocopying and recording, or by any information storage or retrieval system, except as may be expressly permitted in writing by the publisher. Requests for permission should be addressed in writing to LifeWay Press®, Student Ministry Publishing, One LifeWay Plaza, Nashville, TN 37234-0144. Printed in the United States of America

We believe that the Bible has God for its author; salvation for its end, and truth, without any mixture of error, for its matter and that all Scripture is totally true and trustworthy. The 2000 statement of The Baptist Faith and Message is our doctrinal guideline.

Yielded

> **"**Few souls understand what God would accomplish in them if they were to abandon themselves unreservedly to Him and if they were to allow His grace to mold them accordingly.**"**
>
> —*Ignatius*

The Art of

A N ARTIST ISN'T AFRAID TO LET GO.

True artists aren't afraid to give themselves over to the canvas, the clay, the story, or whatever medium they're using. They aren't afraid of the mess they might make or not knowing the ending before they start writing. They just know it's all part of the process.

So, they surrender themselves to the making of art. Artists let go of their tension and fear and embrace whatever direction the piece takes them. Maybe that's the reason art is so hard for some people: it requires us to let go, to surrender—and that's scary, uncomfortable, and full of so many unknowns. So many of us get lost in the questions:

What if I mess up? What if it looks bad? What if I fail?

The Truth about Surrender

Creating something beautiful doesn't require talent so much as surrender. The first step to surrender is desire. You've got to want to create something, want to trust the canvas, the brush, and the process. If you want to let go and simply trust that what shows up on the canvas isn't as important as your needs for perfection or control, then you have taken the first step in the art of surrender.

But that kind of surrender is hard—and surrendering to destructive forces just comes so much easier. It's like the mess in your room; it requires so little effort. All you have to do is nothing—and over time, a mess will appear. And if you don't do anything about it, the mess will slowly but surely take over your entire room.

Ever seen one of those TV shows that profiles hoarders? You know, those people who don't throw anything away because they are afraid of letting go of it or convinced that they might need it someday? Then, because they're emotionally attached to everything, their houses become these cesspools of empty food containers, old clothes, and junk. Slowly, the hoarders get swallowed up by the wave of debris they call treasures. The kicker? When asked, most of these people

Surrender

by Hayley DiMarco

say they have no idea how the mess happened. *It just snuck up on me*, they say. And now, trapped in the mess, they feel powerless to do anything about it. They surrendered their lives to their stuff and soon found themselves victims of that same stuff.

The surrender part was easy; it's the getting free that's hard.

Surrender to God

The absolute truth is that if you surrender your life to anything but God, it will get complicated and very, very messy. Surrender your life to an addiction, and it will rule your life. Surrender your life to impressing other people, and it will ruin your relationships with the people who actually love you for being you. Surrender your life to sin, and you'll end up exhausted, unhappy, and unfulfilled.

But surrendering to God is more like an artist surrendering to her project, just letting go and trusting God to do the rest. Surrendering to God is simple because its requirements are clear: reject everything in your life or attitudes that don't reflect Christ. Simple, right?

Well, actually, that sounds pretty difficult, doesn't it? The truth is, you can't surrender in your own power. In fact, you can't do anything godly in your own power. You might be moral; you might be good; you might even be obedient or come across as a kind and righteous girl, but your life won't truly be godly until you allow the Holy Spirit to lead, inform, and guide every moment of every day.

So, what about you? Are you living according to your own strength or depending daily on the Holy Spirit? Are you trying to live the Christian life by sheer determination? Or are you surrendered to the Spirit—not just for your salvation, but also for your obedience and faithfulness to God?

Galatians 3:2-4 puts it to you this way: "I only want to learn this from you: Did you receive the Spirit by the works of the law or by hearing with faith? Are you so foolish? After beginning with the Spirit, are you now going to be made complete by the flesh? Did you suffer so much for nothing—if in fact it was for nothing?"

Clearly, surrendering to God has nothing to do with your own strength—and everything to do with His.

The Art of Surrender: A How-to

So, you're ready to surrender to God and let the Spirit have control of every part of your life. But how exactly do you do that? Here are some tips to help you in that process:

- **Want it.** There will be no surrender in your life if you don't actually want Him to run your life. Take some time to really evaluate your heart. Do you think you know what's best or trust that God does?
- **Admit you can't.** You can't surrender on your own. But the good news is you don't do it by yourself; the Holy Spirit helps you. So trust Him, and in faith, give God control of your life.
- **Give up your rights.** In order to surrender you have to give up your rights— those things you have determined you should have or should be able to do. These so-called rights are just your own law, and they make you Lord of your life, instead of Christ. Always trying to get your way is really just taking the reigns away from God, who should be in control.
- **Renounce your plans.** Your plans might not be God's plans—and sometimes, you have to give up your plans for His better, bigger plan. Sure, you can plan for things, but when things don't go as planned, don't freak out! Just say "Your will be done, Lord" and trust Him to work things out.

When you surrender to God, you give Him responsibility for your life, your hope, and your future. And you realize a beautiful truth: that you aren't the Artist, but the canvas. You give up your own will for the will of the Father and allow Him, the Creator, the ultimate Artist, to make it into a beautiful masterpiece that brings glory and honor to Him.

WHAT IS SURRENDER?

Surrender is simple if you will just let go. If you still aren't getting it, here are a few more things to remember about the art of surrender:

- **Surrender** means giving up the right to judge God as a bad Father, or at the very least, as a distant one. You trust His plan and His love for you even when you can't see it, agree with it, or feel it.
- **Surrender** means giving up your obsession with the stuff that is happening in your world and grabbing hold of the God that is out-of-this-world. It's letting go of stresses, worries, and fears and trusting God to do what's right.
- **Surrender** means seeing yourself more as a child of God than an individual. That means you recognize that you belong to God and His will is more important than any rights you might have as an individual.
- **Surrender** means you desire God's happiness over your own. It's what draws you toward obedience and faithfulness.
- **Surrender** means trusting that God is all-knowing, all-powerful, and infinite.
- **Surrender** means giving up your right to worry or fear that God will be less than He promises to be.

Have you surrendered?

Have you given up your life or are you still struggling to win? Take this quiz to see if you've given up—and that's a good thing.

What Others Say About You

Circle one word from each line that others would use to describe you:

A. Selfless   B. Defensive   C. Worrier
D. Peaceful   E. Confident   F. Shy
G. Controlling   H. Carefree

- For each time you picked A, D, E, or H, give yourself 3 points.
- For each time you picked B, C, F, and G, give yourself 1 point.

SCORE: ___________

What Your Parents Say About You

Circle one word from each line that your parent(s) would use to describe you:

A. Obedient   B. Disobedient   C. Kind
D. Inconsiderate   E. Troubled   F. Content
G. Selfish   H. Generous

- For each time you picked A, C, F, or H, give yourself 3 points.
- For each time you picked B, D, E, and G, give yourself 1 point.

SCORE: ___________

What You Say About Yourself

Circle one word from each line that you would use to describe yourself:

A. Frustrated   B. Peaceful   C. Trusting
D. Suspicious   E. Obsessed   F. Content
G. Hopeful   H. Depressed

- For each time you picked B, C, F, and G, give yourself 3 points.
- For each time you picked A, D, E, or H, give yourself 1 point.

SCORE: ___________

Total points: ___________

36-30: White looks good on you. You are waving the white flag of surrender. It looks like you've surrendered your life and stopped the battle against the One who's worthy of all of your devotion. Continue to find ways that you can give up your right to yourself and turn your life over to His will.

29-19: Half-hearted surrender. You've given a lot of your life to God, but there are some areas where you just can't let go. When you hold onto those things it might feel like they are safer, but the truth is that it's more dangerous than you know. If you want more faith, more of His presence, then ask Him today where you need to surrender more. Find out the things you cling to for comfort, protection, safety, hope, and joy, and let them go. Lean on Him for all of those things; He can be trusted.

18-12: Throw in the towel. It's time to take a closer look at your life, because right now, your life is all about you. The life of faith changes a girl. It must, or it isn't really faith. If you want more of God in your life, then you have to throw in the towel and surrender your life to Him. Can you trust Him with your life? If you can't right now, then take some time to find out why He is trustworthy and what He will do once you surrender your life—and all your dreams—to Him.

You surrender every day. You yield to the crowd, to the cake on the counter, and to your feelings of guilt. You give your heart over to whatever impulses speak the loudest.

Surrender is simply the act of giving up. Basically, it's giving up the fight to fend off something that threatens to control you and allowing it to have its way with you. Whenever there is ice cream in the house, I say to myself, "I'm not going to eat any because I don't like how I feel after eating two bowls of the stuff." But knowing that a carton of the ice cream is in the freezer pulls at me. It whispers "Hello, there!" every time I walk by. It calls out my name and offers me all kinds of great reasons why I should surrender to its call:

"You've had a long day; you need to indulge, to rest, to let go."

"You haven't had a spoonful of me in two days. What's a small bowl going to do?"

And the barrage of seduction continues until I surrender to the ice cream's sweet promises of relief, sweetness, and satisfaction.

Think about the last week. What are five things you've surrendered to recently? List them below.

1.

2.

3.

4.

5.

You can choose to surrender to anyone or anything that promises you relief, rest, hope, or control. Want rest? You may surrender to the crowd, giving in to their carefree ways and giving up your desire for righteousness, faith, and commitment. Want hope? Yield to the seduction of lust and attention, both of which promise false hope. Want control? Give in to various ways people attempt to feel in control: the relief of the blade, smaller numbers on the bathroom scale, or the urge to purge.

Surrender to that which promises you the most immediate relief or reward, and you will find yourself a slave to it. The world around you and your sinful desires compete with the God of the universe for your heart. All around you, there are voices clamoring for your surrender, so that those needs, desires, and thoughts can be your god, your conscience, and your guide.

You Gotta Serve Somebody

In this world there are two different categories of things you can surrender to: God and everything else. In other words, if you aren't surrendered to God, then chances are you are giving in to the stuff of this world.

And with that kind of surrender comes all kinds of complications. But the stuff of the world isn't just clothes, phones, cars, or guys. It can also include things like fear, worry, doubt, acceptance, and success. Get this, girls: Anything that you surrender to that isn't God Himself is idolatry. And all stuff, once you've surrendered to it, controls you. Like a slave, you obey its call and allow it to steer you, change you, and make you into someone you were never meant to be.

What have you been a slave to (now or in the past)? Check all that apply:

_____ The desire to be perfect in every way (appearance, grades, sports, etc.)

_____ Meeting your parents' expectations

_____ The need to feel good or relaxed (and you may have aided it with drugs or alcohol).

_____ The need to be loved or at least noticed.

_____ The desire not to feel lonely.

_____ Other: ___________________

But the surrender we're talking about here is that moment of surrender when you turn your life over to its Creator. You let go of who you are to become who God wants you to be. You're yielded, ready to let go of your plans and purposes and ready to except His. In this simple act of surrender, you turn over your attempts at control and your lust for comfort and pleasure and choose to place your trust, faith, and hope in the One being who holds the world in His hands.

Unlike the world's kind of surrender, God's kind of surrender is good for your soul, your heart, and your mind. While the other stuff you surrender to chains, abuses, tortures, and controls you, surrendering to God enlivens, emboldens, and frees you from the bondage of sin. If you want that kind of simple surrender, then take this journey with me through this study of God's Word.

Over the next few weeks, we'll be spending some time looking at the lives of a few women from the Old Testament: Ruth, Esther, the Hebrew midwives, Abigail, and Rahab. By studying pivotal events in their lives, we'll come to understand what God can do with a life when He's in absolute control of it.

But before we do, let's examine your understanding of what it means to surrender. Write your definition of surrender below. (Just off the top of your head. Don't look anything up!)

Now, let's take a closer look at the concept of surrender found in the New Testament. Read these words from Mark 8:34-37: "Summoning the crowd along with His disciples, He said to them, 'If anyone wants to be My follower, he must deny himself, take up his cross, and follow Me. For whoever wants to save his life will lose it, but whoever loses his life because of Me and the gospel will save it. For what does it benefit a man to gain the whole world yet lose his life? What can a man give in exchange for his life?'"

Read over that passage a couple of times, then underline all the words or phrases that indicate surrender.

Clearly, Jesus wasn't calling His followers to half-heartedly follow Him or only follow Him when it was convenient or easy. He instructed them to deny themselves, to give themselves up, to surrender. Understand this: we can chase after the things of the world, but they won't satisfy or save us. Jesus has boldly called us to follow Him—and nothing or no one else can save us.

Check out these Scriptures and jot down what they teach you about surrender.

• Romans 12:1

• John 3:30

What It Means for YOU

Surrender is an essential concept in the life of faith. If you have never surrendered to God, you're not a follower of Christ. Without absolute surrender to Jesus, you can't truly worship, pursue obedience, or really walk in faith.

Have you surrendered to Christ? Have you let Him have absolute control over your life or is He Lord in name only? Spend some time thinking and praying about that today. Journal your prayer below.

You have a choice, and no one else can make it for you. You can either surrender yourself to your flesh and all of its desires for this world or you can surrender yourself to His Spirit. God wants to inform, guide, protect, and use you to make this world see His glory and worship His name. If you haven't surrendered your life to Him, it's not too late. God can turn your life around today.

Living a life of surrender isn't easy. There will be times when you will try to wrench control right out of God's hands. But even then, know that He doesn't leave you; He'll be with you every step of the way. As you will come to see through this study, God provides for your surrender.

Just the fact that you want to surrender means He's preparing you for it Himself. So trust Him and dive into the great adventure of simple surrender.

Plan of Salvation

If you're not a Christian and want to start a life of surrender, you must:

- *Acknowledge* you are a sinner who needs a Savior.
- *Believe* that Jesus is God's Son and that He died for your sin and rose again to give you new life.
- *Confess* your sins and turn away from a life controlled by sinful desires. Commit your life to the Lord.

VOICES

AN EXAMPLE

Rahab, Ruth, Esther, Abigail, and the Hebrew midwives are examples because they let God have absolute control of their lives. So, who do you look up to? Why?

"My aunt, Teresa, because we are really close and I can trust her and feel like I can tell her anything and she is a very strong Christian and a great Christian example that I can follow." —*Leah, 13*

"My grandparents and my life group leaders because they love God so much and show me how to live for Him. Also, a high schooler [who is] very close to me, Megan, because she gives us advice on everyday circumstances (how to react in godly ways), and she goes out of her way for others." —*Grace, 13*

"Esther. I admire her courage and bravery." —*Tamara, 17*

COMMITTED TO CHRIST

"Katie Davis (started Amazima ministries in Uganda straight out of high school and has 14 adopted children at age 22) because [of] her desire to care for others and live 100 percent for Christ." —*Amanda, 16*

SURRENDERED

"I look up to Alyssa, a college freshman. She has been a great mentor to me the past year, and she is a great godly woman [who] I try to model myself after. She is such a nice and kind-hearted woman who is living out her life for Christ." —*Haley, 15*

"I look up to my Aunt Brittainy. I think she is such an incredible godly woman, and she has always encouraged me to become all that God wants me to be as well." —*Alyssa, 17*

CONTROLLED BY DOUBT

Dear Hayley,

Recently I've been trying to increase my relationship with God by reading the Bible, listening to only Christian music, and removing myself from bad influences. But I've been still struggling with faith. Lately, doubts have been filling my head, and they just won't go away. It's really scary because I know this isn't good. So could you tell me what I should do, and what is possibly causing this? Because I'm very worried and confused. —*Kina*

Dear Kira,

Know that your struggle with faith isn't the end of the world, and it doesn't change who you are. When you're a child of God, you are a forever child. The Bible tells us that nothing can separate you from the love of God, not even your doubts (Rom. 8:38). Sure, you want to get rid of those doubts, but the way you do it is by trusting God with your faith. He is the one who gives it to you, so He is the one you need to turn to (John 15:16, 2 Thess. 1:11).

When you surrender to God, you end up trusting Him and your doubts fade. So, get to know who God is. I've been where you are, so I know how hard it is. I had so many doubts. But when I found out who God was, how much He was in control, and how much my flesh lied to me, I started to tune out the flesh and trust God completely.

Look up some verses on God's sovereignty and your salvation. Here are some to get you started: John 3:27; Romans 8:29; Romans 9:11; 1 Corinthians 12:11; Ephesians 1:11; Philippians 1:29; Philippians 2:13; and Lamentations 3:37-38.

Most of all: don't let fear have control! God is big enough and good enough to care for you in the midst of whatever you are going through. Trust that He is bigger than anything you could ever face. Praying for you, sister!

WHO'S IN CONTROL?

Dear Hayley,

I get so tired of people telling me what to do. I hate it when they criticize me or try to prove me wrong. I guess I'm a bit of a control freak, but I just wish they would let me live my life and leave me alone. Instead, I feel like everyone controls my life but me! —*Control Freak*

Dear Control Freak,

I have a lot to say about this topic because I'm a control freak, too. I've always struggled with believing that I know best—that I know how to do things best, say things best, and definitely know what's best for me. I play god in people's lives a lot because I'm just sure that I've got it all figured out. Wanting control is essentially believing that you know better than God. Because if God is sovereign and if his Word is true when it says, "A man's heart plans his way, but the LORD determines his steps" (Prov. 16:9), then any idea that you are in control is an illusion. Want to be free from all the pain and agony of always fighting for control? Trust God to be God. The girl who knows that God is sovereign doesn't have to struggle with the whole control thing because she knows who is really in control—not her, not other people, but God. And His control is perfect!

HAYLEY DIMARCO is a best-selling and award-winning author of more than 30 books, including *God Girl*, *Mean Girls*, and *Die Young*. Hayley mentors young women online at *GodGirl.com* and runs Hungry Planet, a publishing company.

KYLA'S CHOICE

A "CHOOSE-YOUR-OWN-ADVENTURE" TALE OF ONE GIRL, THE CHOICES SHE COULD MAKE, AND THE RIPPLE EFFECTS OF HER DECISIONS. by Emily White

PART ONE

Kyla paused for what felt like an eternity, her finger hovering over the screen of her phone. Should she press send?

ONE MONTH EARLIER

Kyla Morris had been a part of her school's Bible Club for the entire time she had been attending Mount Jefferson High. It was well worth getting up early every Thursday morning to meet with more than a dozen of her fellow students for prayer, Bible study, and fellowship. This year, Kyla was co-leader of the group along with her best friend, Nevaeh. And, up until about a month ago, she had always looked forward to those early Thursday morning gatherings.

That all changed when Gabby arrived. A new student, Gabby was incredibly outspoken about the fact that she didn't believe in God. Kyla and Gabby shared several classes and, naturally, their conflicting beliefs had become a popular topic. At first, Kyla had tried to be nice to Gabby and had even shared some of her thoughts about God and the Bible with her. But, over time Gabby had moved from constantly questioning Kyla's beliefs to teasing her about them and, finally, accusing her of being foolish and close-minded. Gabby loudly proclaimed to anyone who would listen that every Christian she had ever met was close-minded, didn't accept people with different beliefs, and—worst of all—was fake.

"They go to church on Sundays," Gabby was fond of saying, "but they don't always act out what they say they believe the rest of the week."

Over time, Gabby's aversion to Christianity had even begun to affect Kyla's involvement in Bible Club. Gabby claimed that it was wrong to have a religious club in a public school, despite Kyla's assurances that the group had cleared it with school administrators before starting the club. But Kyla was growing so weary of the jabs Gabby continued to hurl her way.

Then, it got even worse. A few weeks ago, Gabby had escalated her attacks on Kyla's faith. She'd invited two or three other students to stand outside the door of the classroom where the Bible Club met on Thursday morning. Gabby's small but vocal group mocked the Bible Club members as they arrived and when they left the meeting. Rumors had even begun to circulate that Gabby was spreading gossip about the students who attended the club and was threatening to complain to the school board about them.

Kyla had prayed hard but with all the harassment from Gabby and her friends, was still growing discouraged. Kyla's spunky friend, Addie, had suggested standing their ground and not backing down.

"We have a right to be here!" Addie had insisted. "If we back down or stop meeting we are just letting people like Gabby win! She needs to see that we won't bow to pressure and that we are willing to take a stand for God!"

Nevaeh agreed that standing up for God and doing the right thing meant they were likely to be persecuted. Yet her advice was to reach a happy medium rather than engage in a spirited debate.

"We need to just ignore them and keep doing what we are supposed to do," Nevaeh told Kyla. "Easier said than done, I know. But if we let them discourage us and we stop holding the Bible Club then we miss out on learning and encouraging each other and starting our day prayed up, not to mention the chance to reach other people in our school. I say we move our meetings from the school to the park. We diffuse the argument with Gabby because she can't complain about our meeting in the park, but we still get to hold our club. Everyone is happy."

Kyla was convinced there had to be a third option. She just wasn't sure if it made sense. Addie and Nevaeh both thought she was crazy, but Kyla was still considering the idea. As Kyla mulled over her options she pulled her phone out of her backpack and opened her email. She proceeded to type out the third idea that had been bouncing around in her mind:

Gabby:

I get that you don't like or agree with my beliefs and that I am a part of Bible Club. You talk about not seeing us acting out what we believe or showing God's love. I'd like for you to give me a chance to show you otherwise. I'd love for you to join us this Thursday to see what we are really all about. You're also welcome to go with us next Saturday when a bunch of us are going to go help our youth pastor serve lunch at the homeless shelter. I pray that you'll see what we are really all about.
—Kyla

Kyla read over her message with her finger poised to press the send button. Should she press it? Or should she delete it instead and take Nevaeh's suggestion? Maybe she should just clear this email, follow Addie's advice, and write an entirely different e-mail altogether? Kyla still didn't know which choice was the right one, but she knew that she needed to make one before things really got out of control.

NOW, THE CHOICE IS UP TO YOU. CHOOSE YOUR OWN ADVENTURE:

A. If you chose to send the e-mail, choose ending A.
B. If you choose to press delete and put your phone back in your backpack, choose ending B.
C. If you chose to clear the e-mail and write a new one informing Gabby that you have a right to continue holding your Bible Club and will be standing your ground, choose ending C.

TO BE CONTINUED ON PAGE 122, BASED ON YOUR CHOICE . . .

7 ways you can choose surrender this week

1 Give Up. Choose a possession that you really like and give it away to someone who needs it.

2 Wait a Minute! Before you speak up in class or to a friend, send that text, or watch that show, seek the Holy Spirit's guidance. Let Him lead.

3 Rise and Shine! Write Romans 12:2 on a sticky note and keep it near your bed. Every morning before you get out of bed, read over that verse and ask the Holy Spirit to renew your mind.

4 Let Go. Take a look at your life. Is there something that takes up most of your time, money, or controls your thoughts? If so, take a break from it this week.

5 Night Owl. Every night before you fall asleep, read John 3:30 in your Bible. Ask God to help you let go of control so that more of Christ shines through your life each day.

6 Tough Question. As you make decisions about how to behave, treat others, or how to spend your time, ask yourself this question: *Who's in control: me or God?*

7 Make a Date! Set aside time each day this week to read God's Word and pray. Daily surrender to God in prayer is vital.

ASSU

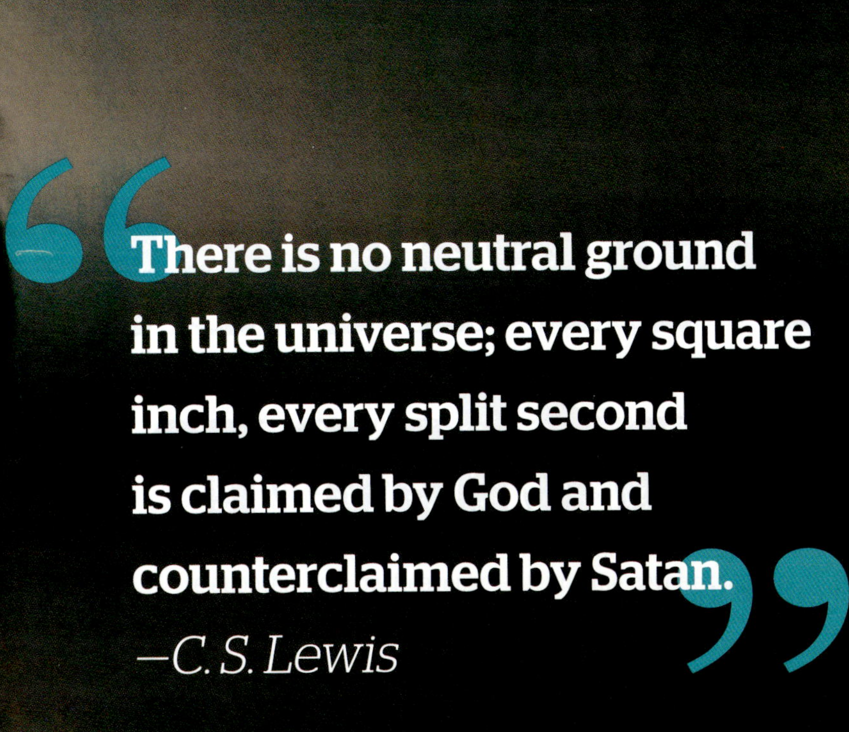

"There is no neutral ground in the universe; every square inch, every split second is claimed by God and counterclaimed by Satan."
—C. S. Lewis

my dad had left I figured that I wasn't good enough to be loved by God. After all, if the perfect man couldn't love me, how could the perfect God?

So I spent my high school years doubting my salvation, believing I just wasn't good enough for it to stick. Every weekend, I would watch my favorite TV preacher and cry, sob over my inadequacies and failures at being lovable. I would beg God to forgive me, to love me, to save me. Every weekend—every single weekend for years—I yearned for God to love me.

I was afraid to trust God's love because I couldn't give up my idea that I was broken and, therefore, unlovable. It wasn't until a few years after my high school graduation that I discovered how God the Father was different from my earthly father. Through a boy who I was chasing, I finally learned that God wouldn't leave me. One day, in conversation, my crush helped me to see that God was different, that once He made me His daughter He would never walk away, never divorce me, and or leave me alone, ever.

"Didn't you know that once you're saved, you're always saved?" my crush asked me.

I was astounded. I stood up in shock and anger and asked that guy how he could possibly know that. He opened up the Bible that he always had with

him and pointed me to Romans 10:9: If you confess with your mouth, "Jesus is Lord," and believe in your heart that God raised Him from the dead, you will be saved.

In a state of absolute relief or pure awe, I dropped down onto the couch. How did I miss that? How did all those people who I had asked about God? How did they miss what I most needed to understand? I needed to know that God was faithful, and no one had ever told me that.

Once I got over my resentment that so many people had failed to tell me about God's amazing grace, I embraced the One who saved me. I took that old Bible that my friend offered me, and I devoured it. I cherished that Bible, because as I read it, the Scriptures answered all my unanswered questions. As a result, I started to pray. I prayed for my dad and my mom, for my friends, and for myself. I surrendered the heart I had hardened in order to protect it from ever getting hurt again. I gave it to the Father who loved me more than I could have ever imagined.

Within a matter of months, my earthly father met my Heavenly Father and surrendered his heart as well. My mother soon followed, as did many of my friends. God not only accepted my surrender, He blessed it. My life has never been the same.

Do I wish that my dad had never left me? I think about that often. Part of me wants to say yes. But the other part of me wants to thank my Heavenly Father, who—though I couldn't see Him or even comprehend Him— was with me every step of the way, leading me to the knowledge of His presence through my suffering. "In this world you will have trouble," Jesus said in John 16:33. "But take heart, I have overcome the world."

Suffering isn't something we can escape as believers. I know that now. We can't escape difficult times, but we can choose how we think about suffering. Today I look at my suffering as a lesson in compassion, an opportunity to experience the same kind of suffering others have suffered so that I might comfort them, teach them, and encourage them.

And as broken as I was on that day that he left, I look at my earthly father as the catalyst that led me to surrender to my Heavenly Father.

"There is no neutral ground in the universe; every square inch, every split second is claimed by God and counterclaimed by Satan."

–C. S. Lewis

red

The Perfect Father

by Hayley DiMarco

When I was little, I thought my dad was perfect.

In my mind, there wasn't anything my dad couldn't do. He seemed to be the strongest man on earth, and the smartest, too. He was a real-life horse whisperer and seemed to know everything there was to know about horses—and he loved to teach me. People came to him to learn about horses, to watch him work, and to laugh. In my opinion, no one was better than my dad.

I loved him. Who wouldn't love the perfect man? Because I loved my dad so much, I wanted to please him. I wanted my dad to be proud of me, and I hated the idea of disappointing him. So, I did everything I could to be perfect. I wanted to be good, to make my dad happy, and get his undivided attention. I followed him everywhere he went. I imitated him, talked about him, and adored him.

When you love someone that much, some interesting things start to happen. You want to please people that you love like that—and pleasing them isn't a burden. Instead, it's a joy, something that you just want to do.

That kind of love also changes what you talk about. What you talk about most is the one you love. All the time, 24/7, your adoration just pours out of your mouth.

Loving someone that much affects how you live your life, too. When you love someone, your love for them often compels you to obey them, too. I loved my dad, and I obeyed him out of that love. I wasn't a good child because I feared punishment; I was an obedient kid, because I was scared of not loving my dad the way he deserved to be. I wanted to please him and never disappoint him.

In many ways, my relationship with my dad shaped the way I think about my relationship with my Heavenly Father. That's why when I think about what it means to surrender to someone, I think about the way I loved my dad. I surrendered everything to him. Whatever he wanted, I wanted, not because he was dangerous and threatening, but because he was wonderful and lovely. My life was joyful, peaceful, and perfect—and I thought my dad was, too.

Until the screaming started.

And then came that day when my parents fought, and my dad walked out. It all came crashing down.

My perfect man was gone, both literally and figuratively.

In one fell swoop, I saw behind the perfect picture of him I'd created and glimpsed into his humanity. For the first time, I saw my dad's sinfulness, his weakness, and his poor choices. I was devastated.

So, I withdrew my adoration and replaced it with hate. I sided with my mom. I changed my name and withdrew from my relationship with him. I changed my life.

For years after that, I struggled with my feelings toward my dad. I tried to deal with all my pain, resentment, and the never-ending questions. Why? Why did he leave me? Why didn't he love me enough to fight for me? How could I have been so wrong in my adoration? How could he?

My understanding of what made someone a good father was shattered when my dad walked out. As a result, it damaged my understanding of who God is. My relationship with my dad had been my example of my Heavenly Father, and all of that was turned upside-down.

My faith was shaken. I believed in God and knew that Jesus was real and exactly who He said He was, but because my dad had left I figured that I wasn't good enough to be loved by God. After all, if the perfect man couldn't love me, how could the perfect God?

So I spent my high school years doubting my salvation, believing I just wasn't good enough for it to stick. Every weekend, I would watch my favorite TV preacher and cry, sob over my inadequacies and failures at being lovable. I would beg God to forgive me, to love me, to save me. Every weekend—every single weekend for years—I yearned for God to love me.

I was afraid to trust God's love because I couldn't give up my idea that I was broken and, therefore, unlovable. It wasn't until a few years after my high school graduation that I discovered how God the Father was different from my earthly father. Through a boy who I was chasing, I finally learned that God wouldn't leave me. One day, in conversation, my crush helped me to see that God was different, that once He made me His daughter He would never walk away, never divorce me, and or leave me alone, ever.

"Didn't you know that once you're saved, you're always saved?" my crush asked me.

I was astounded. I stood up in shock and anger and asked that guy how he could possibly know that. He opened up the Bible that he always had with

him and pointed me to Romans 10:9: If you confess with your mouth, "Jesus is Lord," and believe in your heart that God raised Him from the dead, you will be saved.

In a state of absolute relief or pure awe, I dropped down onto the couch. How did I miss that? How did all those people who I had asked about God? How did they miss what I most needed to understand? I needed to know that God was faithful, and no one had ever told me that.

Once I got over my resentment that so many people had failed to tell me about God's amazing grace, I embraced the One who saved me. I took that old Bible that my friend offered me, and I devoured it. I cherished that Bible, because as I read it, the Scriptures answered all my unanswered questions. As a result, I started to pray. I prayed for my dad and my mom, for my friends, and for myself. I surrendered the heart I had hardened in order to protect it from ever getting hurt again. I gave it to the Father who loved me more than I could have ever imagined.

Within a matter of months, my earthly father met my Heavenly Father and surrendered his heart as well. My mother soon followed, as did many of my friends. God not only accepted my surrender, He blessed it. My life has never been the same.

Do I wish that my dad had never left me? I think about that often. Part of me wants to say yes. But the other part of me wants to thank my Heavenly Father, who—though I couldn't see Him or even comprehend Him— was with me every step of the way, leading me to the knowledge of His presence through my suffering. "In this world you will have trouble," Jesus said in John 16:33. "But take heart, I have overcome the world."

Suffering isn't something we can escape as believers. I know that now. We can't escape difficult times, but we can choose how we think about suffering. Today I look at my suffering as a lesson in compassion, an opportunity to experience the same kind of suffering others have suffered so that I might comfort them, teach them, and encourage them.

And as broken as I was on that day that he left, I look at my earthly father as the catalyst that led me to surrender to my Heavenly Father.

What's your people personality?

Take this quiz and find out if you are more concerned with pleasing others than just being yourself.

The Safety Net:
Trusting God's Sovereignty
by Hayley DiMarco

YOUR BEST FRIEND. YOUR MOM. YOUR BOYFRIEND.

We all have someone we trust the most. It's the person you share your deepest fears with, someone you know you can count on no matter what. Who is that person for you? Write a few names or initials, plus a few reasons you think that person is trustworthy, in the circle.

You need someone you know you can count on in a world where everything around you screams for your attention. Your parents, friends, ads, TV shows, school, Scripture, grades, boys—they're all competing for your attention. List five things that are competing for your attention right now, from the little things, like music on your iPod, to the pressure to be perfect.

1.   4.

2.   5.

3.

With all that noise, it's pretty easy to start to listen to the world and to give into its demands on your life. The world's promises just sound so good—and sin can be very convincing and persuasive. As C.S. Lewis once said, "There is no neutral ground in the universe; every square inch, every split second, is claimed by God and counter-claimed by Satan." You're living in the middle of a war zone where God and sin are fighting for control of your life.

But you're not alone in this battle for control; it's been going on for centuries.

Check out the first chapter of Exodus, if you don't believe me. The Israelites had initially come to Egypt years earlier when there had been a famine. Joseph had been a powerful figure in Egypt in those days, and he'd invited his family to live in his new homeland and share the food he'd stored up in preparation for the famine. (Actually, there's much more to that story. For more, read Genesis 37,39-47.) But then, Joseph died and so did every leader who had known him. And by the time of Exodus 1, the Israelites were completely under the Egyptians' control, living and working as slaves in a foreign land.

The Rest of the Story

Read Exodus 1:8-13 in your Bible. Summarize what happened to the Israelites in Egypt in your own words. Jot down a few notes in the space provided.

Pharaoh felt threatened, fearing the Israelite nation could overthrow him. So, he knew he had to do something about the birthrate of the Israelites. He decided that if he could get rid of all of the baby boys born to the Hebrew women, then within

a few generations their population would cease to exist. It seemed like a good plan.

So, in Exodus 1:16, Pharaoh told the Hebrew midwives, Siphrah and Puah: "When you help the Hebrew women give birth, observe them as they deliver. If the child is a son, kill him, but if it's a daughter she may live."

Read Exodus 1:17 below to see what the midwives did. Underline the reason they disobeyed the king who could have their heads.

"The Hebrew midwives, however, feared God and did not do as the king of Egypt had told them; they let the boys live." —Exodus 1:17

Did you see it? They feared God more than they feared death. Somewhere deep within themselves, they were certain that God was in control and more trustworthy than the most powerful man they knew, Pharaoh. So, the midwives chose to trust their lives to God.

That's complete surrender.

Fear Fuels Surrender

According to Scripture, the midwives refused to obey Pharaoh because they "feared God." Let's take a closer look at what that means.

Look over the following definitions of fear. Check the one that best describes what you think it means to fear God.

- ❏ a distressing emotion aroused by impending danger, evil, pain, etc., whether the threat is real or imagined
- ❏ a specific instance of or propensity for such a feeling
- ❏ concern or anxiety; solicitude: a fear for someone's safety.
- ❏ reverential awe

Sovereign—adjective
possessing supreme or ultimate power; absolute authority and rule of God

Clearly, fear of God isn't the same thing you feel when you see a scary movie. This is reverence or awe, an overwhelming understanding of who God is and acknowledging that He is sovereign.

When studying a biblical concept, it's good to look it up in the Bible in as many places as you can in order to get a better understanding of it. So, let's take a look at some other mentions of the fear of God. Take a look at these verses and write what you learn about fear. Jot down your thoughts, too.

The point? The fear of God isn't a fear associated with punishment, danger, or threat. It's an awe that is rooted in a deep understanding of who God is. It's an acknowledgement that God is in absolute control, all-powerful, and all-knowing. And when you recognize God for who He is, you know that He is absolutely trustworthy. The safety of surrendering to Him isn't that you'll always be safe; it's the assurance that you're always safe in His hands. It's knowing that above all else, God can be trusted.

Once you see how powerful and amazing God is, and how loving He is at the same time, you can't help but stand in awe. The God—who created the universe, controls whether the storms rage or cease, who can give and take life in a millisecond—loves you and has made you His child by giving His Son to die on the cross for you.

Your Turn

Check out Psalm 103:11: "For as high as the heavens are above the earth, so great is His faithful love toward those who fear Him."

Underline the word "faithful" in that verse. God's love is faithful. Unchanging. Steadfast. It's not dependent on what you do or don't do. When you realize that—when you come face-to-face with His love and grace—you want to cherish it for all of your life. When other stuff threatens to take your eyes off of His love, like the Hebrew midwives, you refuse to follow after it because God's love and power are worth so much more.

It can be scary to surrender your life—all your desires, hopes, and dreams—to God, but in that surrender there is safety because He loves you, and He is absolutely trustworthy. It's what the Hebrew midwives understood so long ago.

Flip back to Exodus 1:21 in your Bible and see what happened to the midwives. Because they feared God, He rewarded them. See, your surrender doesn't go unnoticed. Ever trustworthy, God sees, and He promises blessings to those who give up their lives for His sake.

What are the things about God that awe you the most? List a few below.

A Step of Faith: A Modern-Day Profile

by Hannah Wakefield

IN EARLY 2011, Emily had a good job in the publishing industry. She enjoyed what she did and loved her coworkers. She even had written a Bible study for girls that had been published and was doing well.

But then, everything changed.

It all began in a movie theatre in 2009 when Emily saw the movie Taken. After watching the story of the two teen girls who were kidnapped, then forced into the sex trade unfold on-screen, Emily couldn't get the subject off her mind.

"I found myself asking two questions," Emily says. "How many people are actually stuck in trafficking right now? And how many people don't have connections or other means of rescue?"

Emily couldn't shake the feeling that she had to do something about human trafficking. And she couldn't seem to get away from the issue. Her coworkers would make comments about sex trafficking or slavery and Scripture passages about justice that she'd never really noticed before seemed to jump off the pages of her Bible. Emily even found herself reading books about sex slavery.

"It became a heavy burden all the time," she says.

Emily knew she couldn't just sit around while more women were forced into sexual slavery. So, she joined Abolition International, a nonprofit organization focused on eradicating human trafficking and providing aftercare for its victims. There, Emily worked with other women to raise money to minister to the victims of sex slavery.

Yet, it still wasn't enough.

About that time, Belmont University in Nashville, where Emily lived, announced it was opening a new law school. Emily had always wanted to go to law school, and she knew that victims of human trafficking needed attorneys to advocate for them. So, Emily was faced with a decision—stay with her current job or go to work as a lawyer for women who needed someone to speak up for them.

The decision wasn't an easy one. Emily prayed about it a lot, and she had her closest friends pray with her. In the end, she decided to go for it, and she wrote the check to save her spot.

"I remember having the sweetest sense of relief and peace as I wrote the check," she says. "I was genuinely giddy about starting this new chapter in my life."

God has blessed Emily's obedience. Emily has had chances to do internships that will help her career, and she has a sense of focus because she is on a mission to help women affected by human trafficking.

In the Book of Exodus, two Hebrew midwives, Shiprah and Puah, made a decision to save the lives of the Hebrew boys in spite of Pharaoh's orders to kill them. While we know the end of the story (that God blessed them for their obedience), it must have been frightening for the midwives to deliver those baby boys, not knowing what that meant for them. But the midwives still chose to step out and follow the path God had set out for them.

Like the midwives, Emily, who had the comfort and security of a well-paying job and great coworkers, chose to surrender that stability to pursue a calling to justice. She's following an uncertain path, too. She doesn't know where she'll find a job after law school or exactly who she will reach or even if she'll need to live in another country to fight for women trapped in sexual slavery.

But for now, Emily is trusting God and living in the safety that comes from surrendering to Him.

The Hebrew midwives were defiant when they refused to do what Pharaoh said. So, when do you think it's OK to be defiant?

HONOR GOD

When somebody may be forcing you into doing something that dishonors God, because if you say no, you are standing up for your beliefs." —Kayleigh, 14

"When someone tells you to do something you know is wrong." —Beate, 14

"If someone in charge wants you to do something against God." —Amanda, 14

LIVE YOUR FAITH

"I think it is OK to be defiant when you are standing up for Christ. You should only be defiant when you are 100 percent sure you are right, and when you are defiant for Christ, people will see that you are firm in what you believe, and you will not waver in it." —Haley, 15

THE STANDARD

"I think you can be defiant when you are standing up for something that is right according to God's Word. Nothing makes our way of thinking or judgment better than someone else's, but if we base our judgment off of God's standard then I believe that's when we can be defiant." —Olivia, 18

"I think it's OK to be defiant in a situation where I know that it'd be displeasing to God. But also keeping in mind to be respectful about it, especially if it's toward an adult." —Alyssa, 17

WAVING THE **WHITE FLAG** WHEN YOU'RE AT WAR WITH YOUR PARENTS

by Julie Fidler

WHY DID GOD GIVE US THE BIBLE?

Was it because He's a drill sergeant who wants to turn us all into submissive robots with rules and regulations to follow?

No. He had a much better reason. God wants us to know Him. He wants a relationship with us, and you can't have a relationship with someone you don't know and never talk to.

Besides helping us to know God, Scripture also helps us to know how He has called us to live. Most of you would never argue that God is in charge and that we should do His will, but it's harder to say that about your parents. Some of you are cringing right now. You just can't see eye-to-eye with your mom and dad.

Maybe your parents really want you to study journalism at college, but you have your heart set on being a famous singer-songwriter. Not that I know anyone who was like that as a teen or anything. That's a purely hypothetical scenario, OK? (Cough.)

It's true: parents are wrong sometimes. But if you want to have a real relationship with Christ and truly want to do God's will, first you have to submit to your Mom & Dad's will.

BUT IT'S MY LIFE!

It's your life, right? Why should your parents have a say over how you live? Easy. Because God said so.

Don't believe me? Check out Exodus 20:12: "Honor your father and your mother so that you may have a long life in the land that the LORD your God is giving you."

I remember sitting around at youth group one night, debating with my friends about what the word "honor" meant in that verse, because we didn't really want to think we had to actually listen to and obey our parents. If you're like me and you're trying to find a different meaning for that word, here's the Merriam-Webster definition: "to regard or treat (someone) with admiration and respect."

Going against your parents' wishes and arguing until those little veins in your dad's neck stick out—well, that's not honoring your parents. So, how serious is God when He tells us to be nice to our families? Look at Leviticus 20:9 for God's answer: "If anyone curses his father or mother, he must be put to death. He has cursed his father or mother; his blood is on his own hands."

No, God probably won't strike you dead if you say break curfew, and He won't hate you forever if you're disrespectful to your parents. But the point is clear: God means what He says about honoring your parents. Choosing to honor and respect them isn't just a suggestion; it's serious stuff. It matters to God—and it should matter to you.

THE QUESTION: How have you dishonored your parents in the past, and how do you think God would have preferred you handled it?

The truth is, your brain is still kind of figuring things out. Mom might not have a clue how to use an iPad, but her brain is fully developed and yours is not.

While researching a book, a good friend of mine found out that the frontal lobe of the brain—the part that controls judgment and impulses—does not fully develop until after the teen years. Teens tend to rely more on emotion and don't have the skills to make the best judgment calls. Yes, I know you sometimes feel like you know everything, but the truth is, you don't.

So listen when your mom or dad start a sentence starts with the dreaded "when I was your age" phrase. Believe it or not, there's real life experience there—and fully functioning brain chemicals. Just like God, your parents want to spare you some real-life heartache.

THE QUESTION: What decisions have you made out of emotion, rather than listening to your parents' reason? Would it have had a better outcome if you had done what they said?
Take a moment to consider Proverbs 20:7: "The one who lives with integrity is righteous; his children who come after him will be happy."

God will bless you for surrendering to your parents, because when you do, you're ultimately surrendering to Him. Learning to submit to authority, to live by the Truth instead of emotion, and responding in love instead of anger will mold you into the godly person God called you to be.

You will never regret doing the right thing or treating your parents with respect and trust. Best of all, you will bring honor and glory to God in the process.

THE QUESTION: How could surrendering to your parents positively help you to have an eternal impact on your friends?
Think about this: you're arguing with your parents about going to a concert with some non-believing friends but in order to be a good reflection of Christ, you have to say no to the show and respond to your parents in a godly way.

Just because your brain is still developing, that doesn't mean you're exempt from being a godly example to others. You might be the only Christian your friends really talk to, and what you say or don't say can have an eternal impact of your friends' lives.

God hasn't given us authority figures because of some power trip. Being able to surrender to your parents teaches you how to surrender to God, gives you a line of defense against the harm this world can bring, and glorifies God because you're living according to His commands.

So, wave the white flag today. Honor your parents, surrender to God, and trust that He knows what He's talking about—because He does.

Disclaimer: *We're aware that not all parental relationships are healthy or godly. If you or someone else is being harmed in some way by parents or authority figures, absolutely seek outside help. Talk with a trusted adult, student minister, pastor, or godly teacher.*

Trust.
HE'S FAITHFUL AND TRUE.

{ ASK HAYLEY }

HE'S NOT LISTENING!

Dear Hayley,

I have a hard time trusting God when I pray because I don't see Him answering my prayers. How can I pray better so that He will hear me? —*Elisa*

Dear Elisa,

It's important that you first understand that God isn't ignoring you when you pray. He hears you. You just have to learn to trust that His will is better than yours. When you pray, it's important to understand the nature of God. Know that He isn't a bad father who wants to withhold stuff from you to teach you a lesson, but that He wants to bless you beyond your wildest imagination. You just have to trust Him—and surrender your right to accuse Him of not listening. My favorite verse to think about when I feel like God isn't hearing or answering my prayers is Luke 11:11: "What father among you, if his son asks for a fish, will give him a snake instead of a fish?" The point is that God loves you the same way a father loves His child, but in a perfect, deeper way. You may not feel like He is listening or answering your prayers, but trust that He knows what is best for you and is working for His glory and your benefit.

I CAN'T TRUST HIM!

Dear Hayley,

I have a hard time trusting God because things just keep getting worse. How can I trust Him when my life is so messed up? —*Eliana*

Eliana,

I know it can be easy to think that God has skipped out on you when things get bad. But I know from experience that isn't the case. Sometimes, we face difficult times because of sin. In those times, we must admit our sin, ask for forgiveness and repent of it.

At other times, sin may not be the issue. God sometimes uses suffering to bring us closer to Him and make us more like His Son. In either case, your only job is surrender. Give God your heart and choose to trust Him no matter how things look. When you do that, you'll learn more about who God is and why He is absolutely trustworthy.

It may be that you just don't know enough about who God is right now or that you're doubting what you do know. An accurate understanding of God's character won't just change the way you see Him, but it will also change the way you see your life and any suffering you may face. So, if you're up for learning more about God's character, check out these verses: Psalm 86:15; 139:7-10; Isaiah 40:22-23; Micah 7:18-20; John 3:16; Romans 5:8; Titus 3:4-7; Colossians 1:16; and 1 John 3:1.

I have moments when I doubt, too. It's normal. But in those moments, I remind myself of God's character and everything He has done in my life, even through the suffering, and it helps me to see how trustworthy He really is.

HAYLEY DIMARCO is a best-selling and award-winning author of more than 30 books, including *God Girl*, *Mean Girls*, and *Die Young*. Hayley mentors young women online at *GodGirl.com* and runs Hungry Planet, a publishing company.

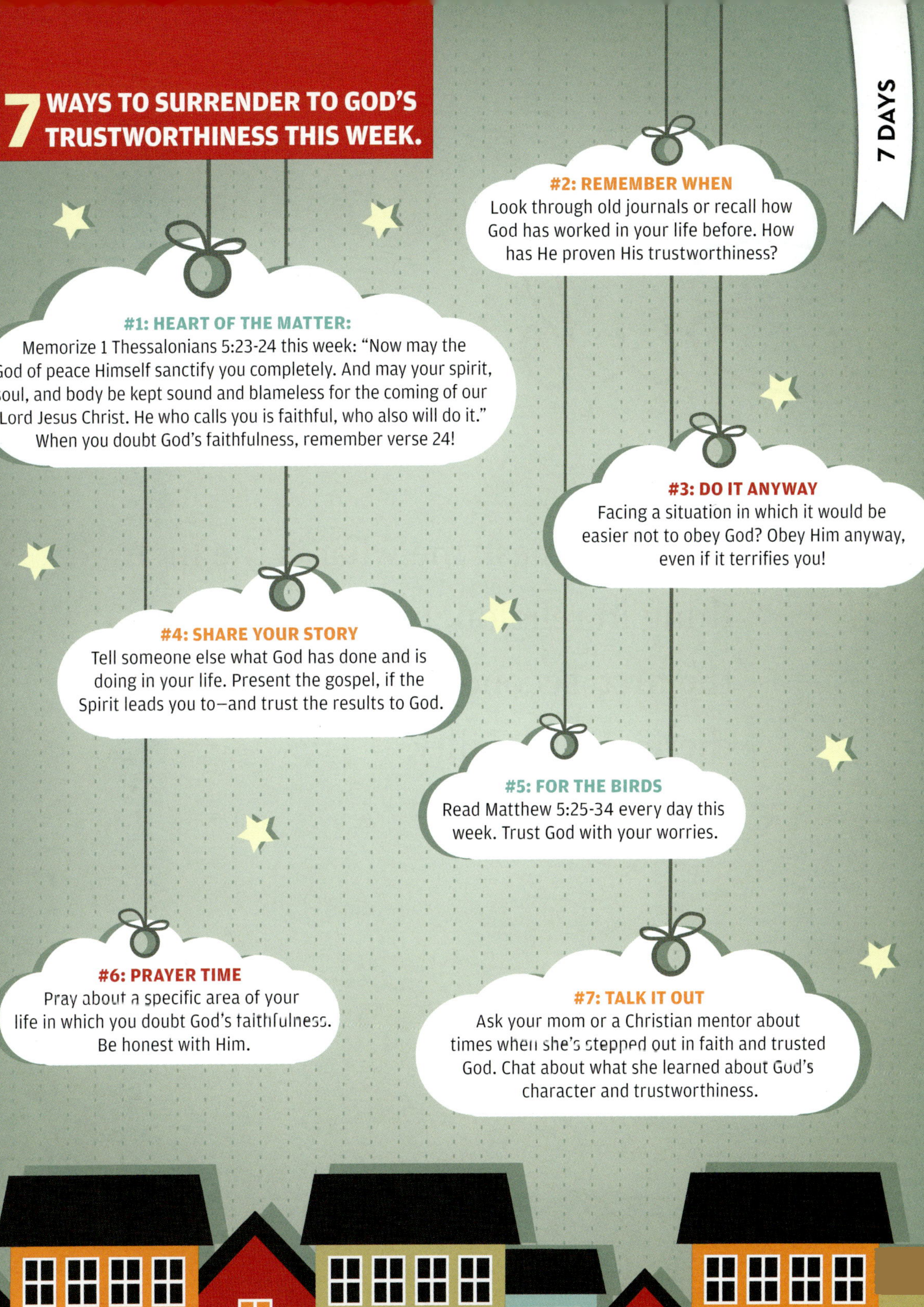

7 WAYS TO SURRENDER TO GOD'S TRUSTWORTHINESS THIS WEEK.

7 DAYS

#1: HEART OF THE MATTER:
Memorize 1 Thessalonians 5:23-24 this week: "Now may the God of peace Himself sanctify you completely. And may your spirit, soul, and body be kept sound and blameless for the coming of our Lord Jesus Christ. He who calls you is faithful, who also will do it." When you doubt God's faithfulness, remember verse 24!

#2: REMEMBER WHEN
Look through old journals or recall how God has worked in your life before. How has He proven His trustworthiness?

#3: DO IT ANYWAY
Facing a situation in which it would be easier not to obey God? Obey Him anyway, even if it terrifies you!

#4: SHARE YOUR STORY
Tell someone else what God has done and is doing in your life. Present the gospel, if the Spirit leads you to—and trust the results to God.

#5: FOR THE BIRDS
Read Matthew 5:25-34 every day this week. Trust God with your worries.

#6: PRAYER TIME
Pray about a specific area of your life in which you doubt God's faithfulness. Be honest with Him.

#7: TALK IT OUT
Ask your mom or a Christian mentor about times when she's stepped out in faith and trusted God. Chat about what she learned about God's character and trustworthiness.

SIMPLE SURRENDER   37

Submitted

> "Should you ask me what is the first thing in religion, I should reply that the first, second, and third thing therein is humility."
>
> —*Augustine*

WHAT HUMILITY REALLY LOOKS LIKE

by Hayley DiMarco

HUMILITY ISN'T BELIEVING THAT YOU'RE WORTHLESS or allowing people to walk all over you. It's making the needs of others more important than your own.

Humility is rare in our world. We live in a culture that is filled with pride and pushes you to do what's best for you, without considering others' needs. True humility is so rare in our world, that when someone lives it out, we find it hard to believe and doubt the motives behind it.

In that kind of world, it's hard to know what real humility looks like. So, that's why I've collected three real life stories of humility and surrender, moments in three people's lives when they laid aside their own dreams, desires, and needs and humbly surrendered their lives to God.

JAMES CALVERT:
My Life Is Not My Own

James Calvert was a missionary in the 1800s. God called him and a group of friends to sail away from home and live with a group of cannibals in the Fiji Islands. They began preparing for the trip and booked passage to Fiji. After a long journey, Calvert and his fellow missionaries finally arrived. A small boat was lowered off the side of the ship to take them to land. As the missionaries got into the dingy and set off, the captain of the ship shouted after them, "You will lose your life and the lives of those with you if you go among such savages!" Calvert boldly replied, "We died before we came here!"

What James Calvert seemed to realize was that his life was not his own. He had humbly submitted himself to God and His plan. He had put to death his own dreams and desires and considered the needs of the Fijians more important than his own. When Calvert got into that boat and headed toward the coastline, he'd already laid his very life in God's hands. In true humility, he had surrendered to God's greater plan.

CORRIE TEN BOOM:
Give Thanks in All Circumstances

Fleas. The place was crawling with them. The rows upon rows of platform beds that filled the Ravensbruck concentration camp barracks were filled with nothing but vermin and straw. And this was where Corrie ten Boom and her sister, Betsie, were living. Most of the ten Boom family had been arrested for helping Jews escape during the Nazi invasion of Holland. Their father had been sent to prison, and Betsie and Corrie were sent to Ravensbruck, a concentration camp in northern Germany. The conditions were subhuman. The girls were packed into rooms with hundreds of other women and forced to sleep body-to-body without even enough room to sit up. The place was crawling with fleas and sickness. There was a putrid odor that hung over everything. Corrie found herself asking her sister how they could live in such a terrible place.

"Show us. Show us how," Betsie prayed matter-of-factly. For Betsie, the distinction between prayer and the rest of life seemed to be vanishing.

Soon, Betsie pointed out 1 Thessalonians 5:14-24 in the Bible the girls had managed to carry into the camp unnoticed. The words of the Scripture seemed written expressly for Ravenbruck: "Comfort the frightened, help the weak, be patient with everyone. See that none of you repays evil for evil, but always seek to do good to one another and to all. Rejoice always, pray constantly, give thanks in all circumstances; for this is the will of God in Christ Jesus."[1]

So, there, in the dark, crowded room, Betsie and Corrie began to thank God for everything in the barracks. They thanked Him for being assigned there together, for their Bible and that there had been no inspection when they entered Ravensbruck. Together, they thanked God for the women in the room who would meet Him in the pages of the Bible and the crowded living situation that would make sure that many more would hear the Good News. Then, while Corrie protested, Betsie thanked God for the fleas.

"Betsie, there's no way even God can make me grateful for the fleas," Corrie said.

"Give thanks in all circumstances," Betsie quoted. "It doesn't say, 'in pleasant circumstances.' Fleas are part of this place where God has put us."[2]

And so the sisters stood between the tiers of bunks and gave thanks for the fleas.

Humiliated beyond what they thought they could bear, Corrie and her sister still humbled themselves before God and thanked Him for the less-than-ideal circumstances they'd been placed in. That's true surrender.

KATIE DAVIS:
It's Not About Me

As her senior year approached, Tennessee teen Katie Davis began feverishly preparing for a trip to Africa. She researched, studied, made phone calls, and worked hard to convince her parents to let her go. At first, Katie's mom was completely against Katie going, but in time, she finally agreed to go to Africa with Katie. So, they set out to serve the children of Uganda. Once Katie arrived in Uganda, she was hooked; she couldn't see being anywhere else. After she and her mom returned from their trip, Katie knew she couldn't go on with the life she'd planned. She set out to convince her dad to let her go back to Africa instead of going to college in the fall. After much discussion, he agreed, with one condition: Katie could only stay for nine months. Katie agreed and set out raising the funds to feed 100 children every day for a year. She needed $3,000 to do it; she raised $26,000!

When Katie returned to Uganda that fall, she began working as a kindergarten teacher at an orphanage. Katie fell in love with those children. She knew that she couldn't just walk away from them when her nine months in Uganda ended. The course of her life changed. Katie had planned for her life to follow a certain path: college, marriage, a job. But it's not the plan God had for her, and she humbly set aside her own dreams to follow His.

Katie moved to Africa permanently. Now in her 20s, Katie has adopted 13 Ugandan girls and started Amazima, a nonprofit that feeds and educates about 2,500 Ugandan children. On March 31, 2007, Katie wrote this on her blog, *www.kissesfromkatie. blogspot.com*: "I have given everything I have—my life, my soul, myself. My heart is entangled in the lives of these children, this mess of poverty, this spiritual joy. I can actually physically feel the hurt in my heart, and as I kiss my daughters goodnight or feel a street kid's tiny fingers wrap around mine, it is almost more than I can bear. But I wouldn't change a minute. If not being quite as involved, not loving with everything I have, not changing lives would eliminate this hurt of leaving, I would choose the pain."

Katie's life isn't centered around her anymore. It's focused on God, His plan for her life, and the girls she has adopted. That's true humility.

Humility is absolutely necessary to surrender. It's that humility before God that allowed James Calvert to lay his life in God's hands. It's what allowed Betsie and Corrie ten Boom to thank God for even the fleas in that crowded, dirty concentration camp where they were treated worse than animals. In humility, Katie Davis surrendered her plans for her life to God and let Him have absolute control.

So, what about you? Will you give it all up for Him? Will you trust Him? You can find all the joy in the world in the most unusual places in the world—in giving up your right to comfort, your dreams, even your very life— when you humbly surrender to God.

Sources

1 Corrie ten Boom, *The Hiding Place* (New York: Bantam Books: 1974), 180.
2 ibid, 180

How Humble Are YOU?

Want to find out where you rank on the humility scale? Take this quiz! Read each statement, then select whether you believe it's true or false.

#1
It is good to put others' needs before your own.
True or False

#2
Revenge is acceptable in some situations.
True or False

#3
It's not OK to compare yourself to others, even if it makes you feel better about yourself.
True or False

#4
Cutting yourself down shows your humility.
True or False

True or False
#5
It is good to confess before you get caught.

#6
It's OK to be proud of your humility.
True or False

#7
If you don't humble yourself, God will.
True or False

#8
Being self-assertive is the only way you'll get ahead.
True or False

True or False
#9
It's OK to not be the best at everything.

#10
Humility means you never stick up for yourself.
True or False

Scoring: Give yourself 1 point for every time you answered true on the odd numbers and 1 point for every time you answered false on the even numbers.

What's your total? _________

What It All Means

0-3 points: Pride comes before the fall. You've got to trust God enough to fight for you. Trust Him and give Him control. When you insist on always being right, you're living for yourself, not for God. Jesus had the right to stand up for Himself, but He didn't because He submitted His will to the Father's. See 1 Peter 2:22-23.

6-15 points: Living a double life. You know that pride is a bad thing, but there are times when people just push all your buttons and you've got to have your say. Open yourself up to the truth that less is more. Read Lamentations 3:31-33 and trust that God will work it all out when you will surrender everything to Him.

16-20 points: On the road to humility. You are well on your way toward humility. It looks like you are eager to surrender your desires to God's. So, keep up the good work and continue to study God's thoughts on humility. (For more, take a look at Rom, 15:2-3; Col. 3:12; Titus 3:2; James 4:6; and 1 Peter 5:5.)

Not About Me: The Humility of Surrender

by Hayley DiMarco

Humility is the act of thinking lower of yourself than of another. It's a modest view of your own importance. It can be painful and doesn't come naturally to us as humans.

And your humility matters to God.

Humility. What's your definition of that word? Is it when you're humiliated? Or some sort of timid weakness that makes you instantly forgettable? Jot down your definition below.

Pride Gets You Nowhere

How do you feel about standing up for yourself? What do you think about the mistakes you make or what other people think about you? All of this has everything to do with your humility.

Humility—understanding you aren't the most important person in the world—is essential to surrender. Without a good understanding of your weakness and God's strength, you cannot—and will not—surrender your life to Him. After all, what do you need God for if you can do it all on your own?

Let's take a look at that concept in Scripture. In 1 Samuel 25, there's a story about David and his interaction with a woman named Abigail. It's a pretty interesting story and has a ton to do with the concept of humility. So, let's take a quick look at this passage. Open up your Bible and read 1 Samuel 25:1-38.

If I had to write a synopsis, it would go like this: Abigail was married to a rich man named Nabal. One day, in the middle of sheep shearing, David's men came to Nabal and asked him to provide them with food and supplies. David instructed his men to remind Nabal of a time when they had provided protection for Nabal's shepherds and sheep. But Nabal flat-out refused, comparing David to a runaway slave in the process. David's men returned to him and reported everything Nabal had said to David. Let's just say David wasn't happy. In fact, he was furious.

Nabal's response wasn't humble. Instead, he responded with arrogance and an inflated sense of his own self-importance. In no way did his response signal submission to or respect for David. Look at the arrow on the next page. As you consider Nabal's response, write the characteristics of a prideful, arrogant attitude inside of it.

Characteristics of a Prideful Attitude

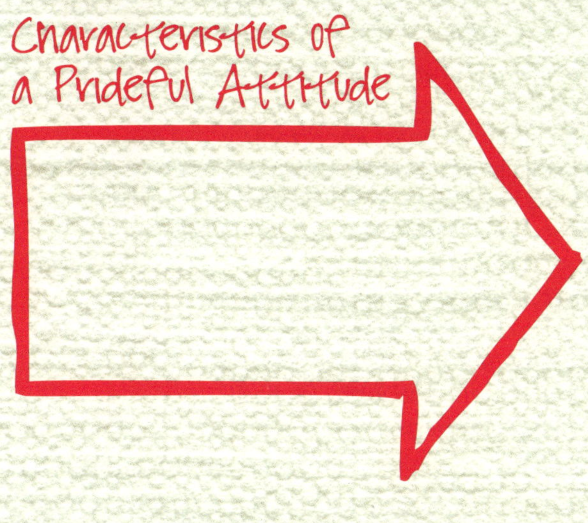

I Samuel 25:18

I Samuel 25:23-25,27

I Samuel 25:26,28-31

Me, Me, Me Isn't Humility

Me. Me. Me. My time. My money. My stuff. What I want. I'm more important than that. Those phrases aren't very humble. And more often than not, when they're a part of your response to someone, they point to an inflated sense of your own self-importance.

For an example of a humble response, check out how Abigail reacted when she heard what had gone down between her husband and David. Read 1 Samuel 25:14-35 in your Bible. Then, take a closer look at Abigail's response in each of the verses listed below. Write your notes about how she showed humility, wisdom, and submission in each instance.

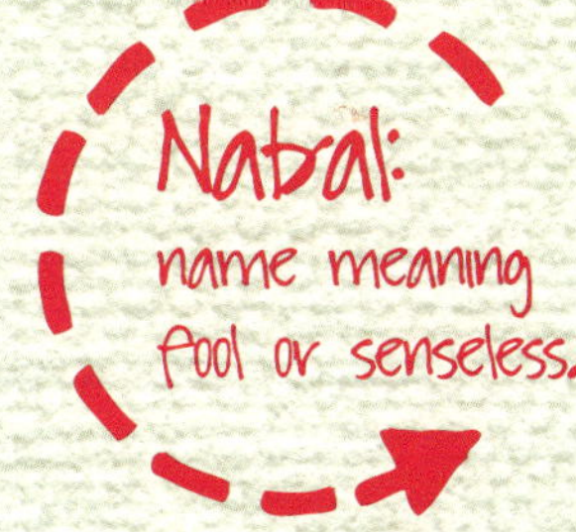

Abigail could have responded to this potentially explosive situation in any number of ways. She could have backed up Nabal and his arrogance. She could have done nothing, claiming it wasn't any of her business anyway. But instead, Abigail responded with wisdom and deep sense of humility, taking Nabal's guilt as her own and calmly and wisely calling David out of his rage by explaining the consequences of David's own potentially rash reaction.

What It Means to You

Abigail could have thrown Nabal under the bus—he pretty much deserved it anyway—but she didn't. Instead, she humbly came before David and took her husband's guilt upon herself. She made herself the least important person in the equation and submitted her very life into David's hands.

Sound like a familiar concept? It should. It's what Jesus has done for us. If you're wondering what absolute humility looks like, just consider Philippians 2:5-8:

> *"Make your own attitude like that of Christ Jesus, who existing in the form of God, did not consider equality with God something to be used for His own advantage. Instead He emptied Himself by assuming the form of a slave, taking on the likeness of men. And when He had come as a man in His external form, He humbled Himself by becoming obedient to death—even to death on a cross."*

Pride–noun

• a feeling or deep pleasure or satisfaction derived from one's own achievements, the achievements of those with whom one is closely associated, or from qualities or possessions that are widely admired • the quality of having an excessively high opinion of oneself or one's importance

Take a look at what these Scriptures have to say about humility and pride. In the space provided, write a few thoughts about what each one teaches you about how you should live.

Mark 10:43-45

Ephesians 2:8

Philippians 2:3-4

True humility is the key to surrender. Jesus surrendered His very life, submitting His will to the Father's plan. He regarded us—you and me!—as more important than His rights as the Son of God. And making our needs more important than the honor He rightfully deserved, He gave it up so that we might be saved.

And Jesus is our example of how to live this life of faith.

Sometimes, in order to understand an idea, it's best to look at the opposite of it. So, let's take a quick look at the opposite of humility: pride. The New Oxford American Dictionary defines pride as *a feeling of deep pleasure or satisfaction derived from one's own achievements.* How might this idea be inconsistent with the life of faith in God?

In the life of surrender, humility is essential. Without it, there can be no surrender. But a lot of times it's easy to lose sight of humility in an attempt to do what seems best to you and make sure things go your way. When that happens, your surrender to God is replaced by your surrender to emotion, self, and sin. Look back at the true/false quiz you took earlier (p. 43). In light of what you have just read about humility, how would your answers be different now?

It's easy for us to think that humility is choosing to think of yourself as worthless. Humility isn't enduring abuse of any kind (physical, emotional, verbal, or sexual) and not sticking up for yourself. It isn't just internalizing whatever a bully says or does to you and never speaking up or telling anyone. Humility isn't ignoring real problems or being a doormat. But, as C.S. Lewis once wrote, "Humility is not thinking less of yourself but thinking of yourself less."

Humility is the opposite of pride and is centered in trusting in God to work all things together for the good of those who love Him (Rom. 8:28). Humility is more focused on God's plans and purposes and fighting for them than fighting for our own plans or rights. Are you ready to surrender your right to fight in order to give your life over to the one who will fight for you?

If you are ready to make that commitment, write a note to God below. Express your desire to submit everything to Him and let Him fight for you, instead of always pushing for your own way.

A Wise Choice: A Modern-Day Profile

by Missy Faulkenberry

God was at work. It was the summer before Kelsey's senior year in high school, and she was at camp with her youth group. And, for the first time, Kelsey had just learned about a summer mission trip to Canada available to students her age.

At first, Kelsey wasn't that interested in going. The trip would be seven weeks during the summer before she left for college. Then, one night Kelsey was hanging out with some of her friends who were seriously thinking about going on the trip. It was in that moment that Kelsey first felt God leading her to go on the mission trip.

It would be hard to give up the summer after graduating from high school, the time when she was supposed to be gearing up for college and enjoying some down time after finally finishing high school. And there were many things to think about when considering an international mission trip: passports, finances, and learning about cultural differences, to name a few.

As her senior year went on, Kelsey made the brave decision to follow God and take the plunge. Her application was accepted, and God paved the way.

But when Kelsey arrived in Canada, culture shock set in. That summer, Kelsey lived and worked in downtown Toronto, and it was abundantly clear that it wasn't the small Alabama town she grew up in. She was shoved out of her comfort zone and forced to go out into the big city and start conversations with people in a way that she had never done before. She had to rely solely on God to give her the strength and boldness she needed to make it through the summer.

While in Canada, Kelsey helped with a food bank, worked with two different churches, and participated in various other ministries. The highlight of her trip was a Vacation Bible School that her group helped with at the end of the summer. Many children heard the saving message about Jesus Christ for the first time during that week.

During her mission trip, God showed Kelsey that wonderful things will happen when she puts her faith in Him and follows Him. She grew in her relationship with God like never before. After she came back home to Alabama, that new maturity helped her to see that are opportunities to serve God all around.

Let Kelsey's story encourage and inspire you. Kelsey learned an important truth that applies to you, too: you don't have to wait to go out of the country on a mission trip to talk to others about God. There are people right in your own community and school that need to know the love of Jesus Christ. Anywhere can be a mission field. Kelsey just started her first year in college and is looking forward to letting God use her wherever He leads.

So, what about you? What is God leading you to do? Maybe God isn't calling you to go on an international mission trip like He did Kelsey, but He is calling you to share His love with others in some way. Will you?

VOICES

Abigail showed great humility and wisdom in her actions toward David. So what in your life do you need the most wisdom about?

RIGHT V. WRONG

"About what the right and wrong thing to do is, because I want to do the right thing but a lot of time for me it's hard to know what the right thing to do is." —*Leah, 13*

"I need the most wisdom right now in trusting the Lord and what He has in store. In making the right decisions and trusting that with prayer [so] I'll be placed where I'm supposed to be." —*Olivia, 18*

DEALING WITH DRAMA

"I need the most wisdom in girl drama. Like how to handle the situations or resolve them." —*Nia, 14*

"I need the most wisdom in my life about what the role of leadership is [for] a woman and patience in the Lord's timing considering relationships." —*Alyson, 17*

"GUYS." —*Ashley, 13*

LIVE IT OUT

"I need the most wisdom about how to live out a Christian life in everything that I do. No matter what I am doing, I want others to be able to see that I am a Christian through my actions." —*Haley, 15*

A GUIDE TO WISE DECISIONS

by Kelly King

Ever play the game "Life"? You roll the spinner and move a car along the road of life's decisions. There are some choices you make—like whether you'll go to college or straight to a career—but most of the game is a matter of chance. According to the game, life sometimes hands you a pink slip. Sometimes, it hands you twins.

In real life, you make decisions every day—and usually it's nothing like "The Game of Life." There's no spinner to reveal the outcome of your decisions about who to date, where to go to college, or what to say in an awkward situation. Instead, your life is based on a series of daily decisions—and those decisions either honor God or rebel against His wisdom.

ALL THINGS CONSIDERED

So, how do you make wise decisions? How can you live a life that honors the Lord and actively seeks Him? Let's take a look at some practical wisdom strategies straight from God's Word, then put them into practice.

Ready?

- **Wisdom begins with respect and knowledge of God's character.** Proverbs 1:7 says, "The fear of the Lord is the beginning of knowledge; fools despise wisdom and discipline." Fearing God isn't being scared of Him. It just means you're willing to yield yourself to His ways and respect His authority in your life.
- **Ask for wisdom.** In 1 Kings 3, Solomon became the king of Israel. God appeared to him in a dream and asked Solomon what He could give the new king. Solomon could have asked for a lot of things, but he asked for wisdom. Verse 12 recounts God's response: "I will therefore do what you have asked. I will give you a wise and understanding heart, so that there has never been anyone like you before and never will be again." And Solomon's not the only one who can freely ask God for wisdom. James 1:5 tells us that if you ask God for wisdom, He will give it to you generously.
- **Wisdom and humility go hand in hand.** The world may portray prideful behavior as a means to wisdom, but God's Word says just the opposite. As Proverbs 11:2 warns: "When pride comes, disgrace follows, but with humility comes wisdom."
- **Lone rangers aren't wise.** Wisdom is found when you seek the advice of godly people and surround yourself with godly friends. Proverbs 13:20 says: "The one who walks with the wise will become wise, but a companion of fools will suffer harm." Who do you go to when you have a decision to make?

Do you seek godly people with life experience and wisdom, or do you ask your friends who may not be as mature or godly?

- **Wisdom is found in people who work hard.** In Proverbs 6, the writer described how diligent ants work and prepare for the future. Verse 6 encourages us to take notice of the ants' hard work and in doing so, "become wise." Do you show laziness when seeking wisdom in a decision, or are you proactive about seeking God's answer?
- **Wise people watch what they say.** Proverbs 10:19 advises us that "the one who controls his lips is wise." Do you consider your answers before actually saying them? Are your words harmful or helpful?

WORD TO THE WISE

You don't just need wisdom for the moment. Yes, you need wisdom when you're deciding what to say when your best friend makes you furious or your parents treat you like a child, but you also need wisdom so that you can live a life that pleases God.

Scripture tells us that you can build your life on one of two foundations: rock or sand. Remember the story in Matthew 7? Jesus told the story of two houses, one built on rock and the other built on sand. Do you remember what happened? When the rains came, the foolish man's house built on sand washed away. The wise man's house built on rock survived the storm. Jesus admonished His followers to build a strong foundation by basing their decisions on God's Word and His teaching.

If you want a life marked by wisdom and godliness, choose to make Christ your foundation. When you face a decision and want to make a wise choice, pray about it. Read God's Word and ask the Holy Spirit to help you understand how it applies to the situations you're facing. Let Jesus be your example and make choices that honor and glorify Him. If Scripture outright rejects one of your options, don't do it. Choose to pursue the things Scripture says are good and avoid those it labels sinful.

Most of all, don't despair if you haven't followed God's wisdom in the past,. While there will likely be consequences for foolish decisions, God's forgiveness is always available. Don't stay on a path that could lead to destruction. Turn around, take the path of wisdom, and follow God's ways. You may not end up with a life of material fame and riches, but God's wisdom has eternal rewards!

BE THE BEST DRESSED.

"Therefore, God's chosen ones, holy and loved, put on heartfelt compassion, kindness, HUMILITY, gentleness, and patience, accepting one another and forgiving one another if anyone has a complaint against another. Just as the Lord has forgiven you, so you must also forgive. Above all, put on love—the perfect bond of unity." —Colossians 3:12–14

© GETTY

{ ASK**HAYLEY** }

IS BEING A PEOPLE PLEASER OK?

Dear Hayley,

I'm a sucker for pleasing people. Now that I'm 15, I am starting to realize that I really have to stop letting people walk all over me! The worst part is, the person who walks all over me the most is my mom. I know I should obey people with more authority—like God, teachers, parents—but I often feel like I'm just obeying her because I want her approval. Should I do things simply because I want to make others like me more? And is it ever OK to say no to something my mom asks me to do? —*Olivia*

Dear Olivia,

Saying yes isn't a bad thing. But if you're motivated to say yes to nearly everything people ask you to do because you want them to like you, that's bad. No one's approval—except God's—should be that important to you. If you've surrendered your life to God and believe that what He thinks is more important than what other people think, then you'll make much wiser decisions.

Now when it comes to parents, God's Word calls you to honor your parents. That means being kind, respecting them, and obeying their commands. So, you have to obey what your mom says—unless she's telling you to do something sinful.

So, if your mom is asking you to do something that isn't sinful but it leaves you feeling like you're being taken advantage of, it's time for a talk. Explain that you're willing to help, but sometimes feel like you've been given too much responsibility. If she understands and agrees, that's great. If not, then you do what God calls you to do: obey her. Let love and obedience motivate you and affect the way you serve your mom, though, rather than anger and hurt feelings. My best piece of advice for you? Do things out of love and not out of a need for approval.

SHOULD I GIVE IT ALL UP?

Dear Hayley,

I saw this documentary on Africa and the starving people there, and it made me sick. They said I could feed 90 kids for a month for just $160! I looked in my closet and realized that I spend that much on clothes. Now I feel guilty because I spend so much money on stuff while kids around the world are dying. I thought about asking my mom to let me send my clothing money to feed the kids, but then what would I wear? Am I overreacting or should I really just give it all away? —*Emily*

Dear Emily,

We definitely overindulge in stuff in this country. We buy whatever we want, eat whenever we want, and forget about the rest of the world. I think it's very noble of you to want to do something to help. I say go for it! How much you send is up to you, but the more the better.

Even though you'll be using your clothing money to help others, you don't have to wear the same clothes every day. Do what you can to shop cheap. Trade with your friends. Plus, you can get some super cute stuff at thrift stores—stuff that doesn't make you look like a clone, but a unique individual.

I encourage you to give away whatever you can. Help whoever needs help. And if you get grief for your less-than-the-latest fashion, just remember that what you're doing honors God.

HAYLEY DIMARCO is a best-selling and award-winning author of more than 30 books, including *God Girl*, *Mean Girls*, and *Die Young*. Hayley mentors young women online at *GodGirl.com* and runs Hungry Planet, a publishing company.

Seven ways you can practice humility this week.

One: Prayer Time.

When you pray this week, kneel. Kneeling is an expression of humility and a physical way to show that you understand that God is holy, righteous, and in control.

Two: Point Person.

Instead of posting about yourself, use your status updates on Facebook, Twitter, and other social media sites to point others to Christ.

Three: By Heart.

Memorize Philippians 2:3 this week: "Do nothing out of rivalry or conceit, but in humility consider others as more important than yourselves."

Four: Be anonymous.

Do something nice for someone in need, but keep it a secret. Stay out of the spotlight.

Five: Serve somebody.

Every day, find a way to serve someone else. Wash the dishes for your mom, do your brother's laundry, or mow your neighbor's yard. Take the focus off of yourself and just do something for someone else.

Six: No comparison.

For one day, refuse to mentally compare yourself to others. Whether you compare to make yourself feel superior or to prove how terrible you are, neither are reflections of true humility.

Seven: Listen up!

Instead of doing all the talking when you're hanging out with friends, choose to listen more and talk less about yourself.

RELEASED

> "Leave the broken, irreversible past in God's hands and step out into the invincible future with Him."
> —Oswald Chambers

OH THE GUILT!

by Hayley DiMarco

Guilt.
From the lie you told your best friend, to that test you cheated on, to that last cookie you ate that you probably shouldn't have.

Do you struggle with guilt and trying to figure out how to get over it? It might be guilt over something stupid you did, or something embarrassing or shameful—but no matter what, it's hard to get it out of your mind. *How could you? Why did you? And will God ever forgive you?*

Guilt changes a life. In fact, guilt can destroy a life. There are tons of girls who have done things they said they'd never do out of guilt. They've hurt people, given too much of themselves away, lied, cheated, and stolen. They've cut themselves, thrown up, and starved themselves. Because of guilt over their past, many girls have grown into women who truly believe they should never truly be happy because of who they were or what they did.

Guilt can mess you up.

GOOD GUILT

But it doesn't have to be that way. It's important that you understand what guilt is and what it's meant for. (Yes, guilt is meant for something.) Good, old-fashioned guilt is meant to be a red flag, a warning sign, something that wakes you up and brings you to your senses. Guilt is meant to do one thing and one thing only: to convict you of sin. Your guilt is meant to lead you to a place where you can acknowledge that what you did was wrong and agree with God that it was sin. Good guilt is synonymous with conviction; it leads you to repentance. It's meant to lead to a change in your life.

BAD GUILT

But there's also such a thing as bad guilt. Maybe you really messed up with God. You lied; you slept with your boyfriend; you sinned. Over time, the Holy Spirit convicted you of that sin, and you went to God with your guilt and shame and asked for forgiveness. You repented and walked away from that sin for good—but even now you still feel guilty about it. So, you confess it over and over again, begging God for forgiveness, pleading for Him to set you free.

If that describes you, understand this: when you truly confess your sin and turn away from it, God forgives you. Completely. Instantly. He forgives you as soon as you confess. So, those feelings of guilt and shame that you feel even after confessing and turning away from your sin aren't examples of good guilt. They're just an ugly imitation of it. You have to trust God at His Word in 1 John 1:9: "If we confess our sins, He is faithful and righteous to forgive us our sins and to cleanse us from all unrighteousness."

You are no longer sinful after you confess your sin. Period. The end.

But sometimes, if you're like me, you may feel guilty for things you've done, said, or decided that aren't sinful. Maybe a friend asked you to do something, and you said no because you already had plans. Then she got mad, and you felt guilty for letting her down, even though you'd done nothing wrong. It's easy to feel guilty when you feel like your answer has let someone down or caused disappointment or disapproval, but saying no to something—unless it's something God says for you to do—isn't a sin. Scripture has a lot to say about what is and isn't sin. Pay attention to the Bible and the conviction of the Holy Spirit, and live accordingly.

WHAT IT MEANS FOR YOU

If you are feeling the brokenness of a life polluted with guilt over past sin that you've already repented from, then let's put that lie to rest. Your life never has to be polluted with your past as long as you confess your sin to God, repent from it, and trust He is big enough to forgive. Understand that once God has forgiven you, your sin is gone, "as far as the east from the west" (Ps. 103:12).

Sometimes, it isn't guilt from old, already-forgiven sins that haunts you; it's guilt from recent sin. The next time the Holy Spirit uses guilt to convict you of sin, ask yourself these four questions:

- Did I sin?
- Do I want to confess?
- Can I trust His forgiveness?
- Do I want to repent?

If you can answer yes to all four questions, you're in a good place. Confess your sin to God as soon as the Holy Spirit makes you aware of it. Truly repent and turn away from it. Then, trust God's forgiveness. You never again have to be plagued with feelings of guilt, because Jesus took on all of your guilt—past and present—when He died on the cross. As it says in 1 John 2:2: "He Himself is the propitiation for our sins, and not only for ours, but also for those of the whole world."

To put it simply, when Jesus died on the cross, He put your sin to death, too. All you have to do is accept His free gift of salvation. Your guilt is gone. He took all of your sins—all of them. And the new life He gives you takes your brokenness and blesses it.

Let Him set you free from guilt and shame today.

Where's your focus?

Are you living life looking in the rearview mirror and letting your past define you? Or, are you living in the power of God's redemption and amazed at how He's shaping your future? To find out, take a look at the columns below. Compare the phrases in each column, then circle the one that best describes you.

That  OR

I feel broken, but I'm not hopeless.

I want to please God.

Other people are more important than me.

I have taken responsibility for my past and my sin, but I live guilt-free.

I strive to forgive people when they hurt me.

I leave revenge to God.

I know that I can't earn God's love, but accept it still.

I choose to trust God's forgiveness.

I am a glass-is-half-full kind of person.

I am content with my life.

Total circled in this column:_____

This

I feel hopeless and broken.

I am a people-pleaser.

I deserve better than others.

I'm wracked with guilt about my past or my sin.

I resent someone who hurt me.

I want revenge on someone.

I am worthless.

I have tried to punish myself for my past.

I am a complainer.

I get jealous easily.

Total circled in this column:_____

If most of your circles are in the "That" column:

Wow! The way you think about yourself, your past, and God are in line with the brokenness of surrender. You probably didn't circle everything in the "That" column, but that's OK. Take time to look over the phrases you circled in the "This" column, though. Are you striving for control, your own happiness, or perfection in any of those areas? Choose to surrender those things to Him. It's time to surrender everything!

If most of your circles are in the "This" column:

There is a lot of brokenness in your life, but you may not be trusting it completely to Christ and allowing Him to work in all areas of your life. If you want to experience more of the fruit of the Spirit in your life—more love, joy, peace, patience, kindness, goodness, faithfulness, gentleness, and self-control—it's time to center your thoughts and the way you think about yourself and your past on God, rather than yourself. God can truly make you whole. When your past threatens to overwhelm you, remember the story of Paul, who persecuted Christians before becoming a Christ follower. He could have majored on his mistakes and made himself miserable about the facts of his past, but instead, he focused on Christ's victory. Putting the past behind him, he followed hard after Christ.

Released: The Brokenness of Surrender

by Hayley DiMarco

Useless. Pointless. Hopeless. Unsalvageable.

We think that if something's broken, then it must be useless. When a relationship falls apart, we move on to new ones. In a world of broken dreams, broken hearts, and broken promises, it's pretty easy to believe that the broken pieces can never be put back together again.

In our world, broken things are useless. And when you're the broken person, it's easy to think that you're useless, pointless, and beyond hope, too.

But that's not the way God looks at brokenness. To Him, our brokenness isn't the end of the road. It's the beginning. In the life of surrender, brokenness is essential.

All the Broken People

The Bible is an anthology of brokenness. Think of Hannah crying broken-heartedly as she prayed for a child. There was David, who committed adultery and arranged for a man's death. Abraham, the patriarch of the faith, lied when push came to shove and made some pretty poor decisions along the way. Peter denied Christ. And Paul, whose letters comprise much of the New Testament, made a name for himself persecuting Christians.

Throughout the pages of Scripture, you find the stories of people whose lives seem broken beyond repair. And even so, God didn't reject them. In fact, many became important figures in His plan.

One of those people is Rahab. She made her first appearance in Joshua 2. Let me set the scene: The Israelite spies had come to do some recon on Rahab's city, Jericho, and were about to be captured, so she hid them. Rahab was a prostitute, a woman who made her living in a profession based on sin and lust. If anyone's life could be described as broken, hopeless, or too far gone, it was hers. Surely, the very last person God would use for anything would be someone with a past as messed up and sinful as Rahab's.

Wrong! Turn to Joshua 2 in your Bible and read it in its entirety. Record the highlights on the timeline.

Want to know the rest of the story? Take a look at Joshua 6:17: "But the city and everything in it are set apart to the Lord for destruction. Only Rahab the prostitute and everyone with her in the house will live, because she hid the men we sent."

Rahab hides the spies

Spies promise to remember Rahab

Why Her?

Why would God care about Rahab? She wasn't even an Israelite. Rahab was a pagan woman who lived a lifestyle that openly defied what God valued. Yet God not only protected her, He also made her a part of the line of David. Just check out Matthew 1:2-6. Rahab the prostitute—the broken woman with a past that seemed irreparable—became an important figure in the lineage of the Messiah.

Let that sink in.

Scripture doesn't outright tell us why God honored Rahab, but we can draw some important conclusions about her character from her responses recorded in Joshua 2. Ready?

1. Rahab heard and believed (Josh. 2:10). Rahab told the spies that she and everyone in the city had heard about all that God had done for the Israelites, the miracle of the Red Sea included. She hadn't seen it with her own eyes or walked across the dry riverbed with walls of water on either side of her. But she had heard what God had done, and she believed. She had faith, even when it seemed improbable or hopeless.

2. Rahab recognized God for who He is (Josh. 2:11). Check out Rahab's bold statement in Joshua 2:11: "for the Lord your God is God in heaven and on earth below." Rahab, as messed up as her life may have been, recognized that this was the one and only God who was sovereign over all the earth.

3. Rahab placed her trust in God (Josh. 2:12). Despite growing up in a society that didn't revere God, Rahab asked the spies to swear to her by the Lord that they would spare her life and the lives of her family members. She had grown up in a society that worshiped many gods, but when her life depended on it, she didn't turn to those gods. She placed her trust in the one true God.

What It Means for YOU

Ever felt a little broken or hopeless yourself? Does your past feel like a heavy burden? Have you ever been absolutely convinced that your life is too far gone for God's redemption?

When you feel broken and beyond restoration or redemption, remember Rahab. Recall how God released her from her past. In the middle of your hopeless situation, do what Rahab did: remember that God is exactly who He says He is.

A Reminder

When you see a blank line, insert your name.

I, _____________________, know what God can do, and I believe,
even though I feel hopeless right now. When the weight of my
past threatens me or I feel like I'm drowning in the guilt of my
confessed sin, I, _________________, will recognize God for who
He really is: my Father, my Creator, my Savior, sovereign over all
the earth. Even though I'm scared, I, _______________, will place
my trust in God. He has a plan for my life, and through His Son,
He has redeemed me from all my sin.

Beautifully Broken

Because brokenness is important to God, it's a recurring theme in
Scripture. Look up the following verses in your Bible. Jot down a few
notes about what each one teaches you about brokenness.

Understand this: God will take your brokenness and make something beautiful from it. It's what God does. Brokenness doesn't exclude you from great works—it almost assures them, as long as you are willing to surrender your pain, suffering, and even your mistakes to Him.

God did it in Rahab's life, transforming the pagan prostitute into a woman who would be in the lineage of the Messiah.

He also did it in Paul's life, releasing a man weighed down by the weight of his past with the power of salvation.

Consider 1 Corinthians 15:9-10: "For I am the least of the apostles, unworthy to be called an apostle, because I persecuted the church of God. But by God's grace I am what I am, and His grace toward me was not ineffective. However, I worked more than any of them, yet not I, but God's grace that was with me."

God clearly used Paul despite his broken, messed-up past. He can use you, too. It's time to lay it down, let it go, release it, and be released.

Ask Yourself

- Why did Paul think he was "the least of the apostles"?
- God uses Paul despite his brokenness. Do you have any brokenness in your life that you feel is holding you back from surrendering to God?
- Knowing what He did for Paul, can you see that God is loving enough to accept your surrender as well? Why or why not?
- According to this verse, how was Paul able to surrender and to work harder than others? What does that mean?
- How do you see God's grace working in your life?

How to Be Set Free

Your sin is real (Rom. 3:10). But you aren't alone. We're all in the same boat. And we will continue to sin, fail, be rejected, and make some stupid, sinful choices, but we don't have to remain broken. God wants your surrender so that He can change your life into something more beautiful than you ever dreamed. Want to be released?

1. **Admit your brokenness—and your sin.** Make a list of your offenses and confess them to God. Agree with Him that you have sinned and take responsibility for your sin.
2. **Trust Him.** Trust God to be true to His word and to not only forgive you, but to also redeem you. God doesn't accept the prideful who boast in their purity and holiness, but He reaches out for the humble who recognize their brokenness and eagerly accept the redemption offered in the sacrifice of Jesus Christ, his Son.
3. **Surrender.** Let go of your brokenness and sin, then choose to walk in another direction, knowing that God will make something beautiful from your surrendered life.

RESTORED:
A MODERN-DAY PROFILE

by Hannah Wakefield

This is not my story," Amy Austin is quick to say when she talks about her life. Her point is clear: her life is God's story of redeeming her past.

Amy's earliest memories consist of parents who communicated mostly through yelling and swearing. Her mother is bipolar and struggles with a drug addiction; her dad has mental and emotional challenges. As a child, Amy remembers feeling neglected and abused.

"Often, strangers would threaten our family," Amy say. "And it was not uncommon to have police checking up on 911 calls that either came from our home or neighbors."

Thankfully, Amy's grandmother was a bright spot in her childhood. At her grandmother's house, Amy saw that a relationship with God led to a life of hope and peace—a life that she wanted. When Amy was 12, her grandmother signed her up for a summer camp. During that camp, Amy heard God speaking to her heart for the first time and believed in Him.

But at the same time, many other things were pulling Amy further away from God. Stranded alone at a house with guys who were drinking and doing drugs, Amy was sexually abused by one of the guys. That led to a new, dangerous mind-set for Amy.

"I thought that people were going to take what they wanted from me, and I couldn't control it," she says. "So, I had to figure out what people wanted and give it to them before they could force me."

Amy became addicted to alcohol and cocaine, and her life spiraled out of control as she tried to please everyone. Amy would cry out to God to rescue her every night. Then, Amy's grandfather reminded her of something her grandmother had always believed: that the Lord had something more for Amy than the kind of life she was living.

With those words, God offered Amy hope. So, when she was 14, Amy signed herself into the Tennessee Baptist Children's Home. That day, she found a Bible lying on her new bed, so she picked it up and started reading. "James, a servant of God" were the first five words she read.

Amy says that those words didn't just change her life; they saved it.

In that moment, Amy recognized that she wasn't defined by her past. She was a servant of God. Her life was no longer about pleasing people, but surrendering to God.

At the children's home, Amy's house parents taught her how to know God and follow Him. Eventually, Amy became the first person in her family to graduate from a four-year-university. Today, Amy is happily married to a godly husband. She serves as the spiritual life director at a Christian school, is getting her Master's degree in marriage and family therapy, and choosing to surrender daily to the God who continues to restore her.

Voices

Rahab's past wasn't perfect—and probably full of regrets and things she wished she could change. So what do you wish you'd never done?

"Put my worth in a boy's opinion." —*Alyson, 17*

Trust Issues

"Over-think things. This may sound stupid but . . . there [are] nights where I think so much about something that I somehow make myself disprove something I know to be true instead of just trusting in the Lord." —*Olivia, 18*

People Pleaser

"Cared what people thought of me." —*Grace, 13*

"Compromised myself." —*Tamara, 17*

"Doubted God." —*Morgan, 13*

What's Really Important

"Done so many sports this past year because I didn't have the time I needed to grow as much as I would have liked to in Christ and go to Bible studies and such." —*Carlyn, 15*

Three Days that Changed My Life

(AKA How I learned to forgive)
by Dawn Cornelius

There are essentially three days that have profoundly changed my life forever.

THE FIRST DAY was the day my mother abandoned me and my twin brother in a local hospital at birth. Although I was an infant and unaware of what was happening, this fall day in 1972 would serve to shape the rest of my life. It would become the beginning of a torrid journey toward forgiveness, self-worth, and discovering my purpose.

My biological mother became pregnant with me and my brother while she was married to an alcoholic and abusive husband—who wasn't my father. She already had four other children. The youngest was 5 years old, and her oldest was 10. Once my mom's husband discovered her pregnancy, he threatened to kill her if she didn't abort the baby—neither of them knew at the time that she was pregnant with twins. But since you're reading this article, you already know that she chose to give us life.

I've spent much of my life replaying that day. What was the weather like on the day I was born? Who went to the hospital with my mother? What was she thinking when she first laid her eyes on me? Did anyone realize that this day would unlock bitterness, resentment, sometimes hate (mostly me hating myself), and every other negative emotion associated with abandoning a helpless, perfect newborn in a dusty, dim hospital where only people without health insurance and financial stability gave birth? Did anyone say "Congratulations Mrs. _______? Or did everyone just smile politely, drop their heads knowing that one more statistic had been born into a life of poverty, disdain, and limited opportunities?

Meanwhile, my father had not pledged any support to my mother and actually denied to everyone that he was our father. I can only imagine how alone, helpless, and hopeless my mother felt. My father began to conspire to convince others—mostly young adult, single female cousins—to adopt my brother and me. Those plans failed. But, finally he did manage to convince my grandmother (his mother) to visit my brother and me, who he described simply as newborns who had been abandoned at the local hospital.

CUE THE MUSIC. One crisp, fall day after being convinced by her son to visit us, my grandmother went to the hospital without any grand plans but certainly with an open heart.

This would be the second day that would change the entire trajectory of my life. I have always imagined my 65-year-old grandmother arriving to the hospital early that morning with a slow, yet steady stride earned from long days working in the cotton fields of southern Alabama, hands tough from honest labor, eyes that are steady and intense from seeing injustice, and a countenance that radiated with compassion because of her deep, rich faith. I have probably imagined this day as much, if not more, than the day I was born because on this day, hope was born in my life.

I wonder what my grandmother thought about as she walked through those halls approaching our cribs. She had no idea that we were, in fact, her biological grandchildren. So, it wasn't salvation of another generation that compelled her; it was the love of God that moved her to reach down into each of our cribs and see the potential and possibilities in our eyes and motivate her to place us in her purse and take us home.

Unbelievable, but true.

Her decision profoundly changed my life. She didn't just save us from a life of foster homes, orphanages, and state custody. She gave us access to a life of opportunity, exposure to a living example of God's Word, and introduced us to Christ Himself.

We didn't grow up privileged. Actually, the opposite was true. We grew up in abject poverty, lived in the inner city, and weren't afforded any of life's excess privileges. Yet, I feel as if I had the richest of childhoods because of the values I learned from my grandmother: sacrifice, God's amazing love, hard work, diligence, the power of education, humility, diversity, believing in people, never giving up, knowing that anything is possible, valuing others regardless of class or culture, shared responsibility, and community. 1907 was the year my grandmother was born; it's the year my hope was born, too.

When I was 16 years old, I met my biological mother for the first time. My father had made her promise that she would never tell us who she was, so she had no idea that we knew her true identity. On one of her visits back to the city where I lived, she dropped by our home. I was happy to meet her and had envisioned this moment so many times.

It was awkward at best. I could feel the tension, her shakiness, and knew she was wishing she could blurt out her true identity but was frightened by the possible scorn I might inflict.

During that visit, I managed to get my mom's contact information from one of her children, a sibling I'd never seen in my life. Very quickly after this visit, I wrote and mailed my mom a letter. (Email wasn't born yet!)

Days later, my mother called. That call was full of all the emotions you can imagine: sadness, laughter, and nervousness, all rolled up in one. My mother began explaining her decision from 16 years prior. Sobbing and often inaudible, she tried to make sense of the years of hurt, the feelings of abandonment, my self-hate and low self-esteem, and, most of all, the deep, abiding and unfulfilled longing I had for the woman who birth to me.

I'm not even sure how far she made it into her explanation when a profound truth came to mind. On that day, I said this to her: "I really don't know what happened 16 years ago, and I'm not even sure anyone can change it or if it even matters now. It's done now. But, the only day we have is today. I forgive you for what happened 16 years ago, and the only day that matters to me now is today. I give you today."

It was truth then, and it's truth today.

The short story is this: my mother was never able to make good on that deal. She always struggled with it—and that would only serve to further disappoint me and cause deep hurt. But, that day on the phone all those years ago was a life-changing day. When I extended forgiveness to my mother, it would begin a journey of forgiveness that would set me free. It didn't happen overnight. As a matter of fact, it would be nearly seven years later before I could fully embrace the gift and joy of forgiving someone else in my life.

Forgiveness is a decision. It's not an emotion. It's a decision that in time will affect your emotions. Forgiveness doesn't let the person who wronged you off of the hook or protect them from the consequences of their actions. It doesn't even mean that you will spend the rest of your life in relationship with them. You may never be in a healthy, thriving, restored relationship with that person ever again. But if you want hope, grace, goodness, mercy, and possibilities to be born in your life, forgiveness is the only way to do so.

What I told my mother that day on the phone is true: the only day you have is today. Let God set you free to forgive and allow hope to be born in your life.

DON'T LIVE YOUR LIFE IN REWIND.
THE PAST IS OVER.

"But one thing I do: Forgetting what is behind and reaching forward to what is ahead, I pursue as my goal the prize promised by God's heavenly call in Christ Jesus."

—Philippians 3:13b–14

©GETTY

{ ASK HAYLEY }

I CAN'T STOP!

Dear Hayley:

I used to cut when I would get upset with myself. I stopped because I thought it was wrong and I hated doing it, but lately I've started to cut again. I feel like punishing myself, but I'm scared that I'm going to hurt myself. How do I stop doing this and get God to forgive me? —*Danielle*

Dear Danielle,

I know that when you cut you feel like you get some relief, or that it makes you feel better. But the cost is more than you might even know. When you cut to fix things, to punish yourself, to get some kind of control in your life, or just feel something other than terrible emotions swirling around your head, you're living a lie. The lie is that you are trying to fill in for God's failure. You say you cut because you're upset with yourself—but it's God's job to judge the innocence or guilt of all people (Ps. 75:7; 2 Cor. 5:10; Jas. 4:12). When you take that job on yourself, you're not only attempting to take God's place by judging yourself; you're also accusing Him of not doing what He ought to do.

Thinking that you need to be punished for something can be a symptom of guilt. Whether it's genuine guilt because of a real sin or imagined guilt because of a bad feelings, the prescription isn't punishment, because there is no punishment for the believer (Rom. 8:1; 1 John 4:18). The prescription is forgiveness, a forgiveness that you don't give yourself, but that God gives you.

Trust that God is enough. If you need more ammo to fight this battle, check out these verses:

- Romans 3:32-26
- Romans 5:8-11
- Titus 3:5
- James 5:16
- 1 John 1:9

FORGIVE ME

Dear Hayley,

Lately, I've been feeling God is very distant from me. I did some really bad stuff, and I just can't forgive myself. How do I forgive myself when I can't seem to forget what I did? —*Sierra*

Dear Sierra,

I've got good news: you don't have to worry about forgiving yourself. Really, the only kind of sin is sin against God. So when it comes to forgiveness, it isn't yours that you need; it's God's.

Read Psalm 51 in your Bible. When David sinned he acknowledged that he had sinned against God and God alone (Ps. 51:4). The rest of that psalm is David's confession to God. What David knew—and you need to know—is that God is quick to forgive, faster than humans in fact. He, in all His righteousness and power, forgives you as quick as you can confess that you sinned. When He forgives you, you are absolutely, completely, and truly forgiven. The only thing to do, then, is to get over it.

If you've truly confessed your sin to God and asked for His forgiveness, you're forgiven. You don't have to feel guilty for it any longer. It can be a long process to get over something, but each time you feel the pangs of guilt, remind yourself that God has forgiven you and take the opportunity to praise Him, rather than relive your mistake. Soon, you will be set free even from the ugly memory.

HAYLEY DIMARCO is a best-selling and award-winning author of more than 30 books, including *God Girl*, *Mean Girls*, and *Die Young*. Hayley mentors young women online at *GodGirl.com* and runs *Hungry Planet*, a publishing company.

7 ways you can let go of your past this week.

#1
Metamorphosis.

Memorize 2 Corinthians 5:17: "Therefore, if anyone is in Christ, he is a new creation; old things have passed away, and look, new things have come." When past guilt and shame creep up, remind yourself that you're made new in Christ.

#2
Write It Out.

Is there someone you need to forgive? Are you holding a grudge? Ask God to help you forgive that person. Write a letter to him or her, even if you don't know how to contact them anymore, and extend your forgiveness.

#3
No Rewind!

Refuse to live your life always looking back. Press forward! Write Philippians 3:12 on your mirror in dry erase marker. Read it every day as you get ready.

#4
Make a List.

Yes, your past was bad, but it's likely God was at work. Think about your past and list 25 things you're thankful God did, even when you were at your worst.

#5
Change Your Mind.

Take note of how much you think about past mistakes or painful experiences and when they come to mind most often. When they do, remember Philippians 4:8 and set your mind on the things of God.

#6
Tell the Truth.

Talk about your past—sin, painful experience, whatever—with your mom, a trusted Christian mentor, or friend. Ask her to pray for you as you struggle to move past it

#7
Stand Firm.

When past guilt and shame threaten to overwhelm you, remember who God says you are if you're His child: beloved, made whole, and righteous.

Sacrificed

> "Don't force me to leave you; don't make me go home. Where you go, I go; and where you live, I'll live. Your people are my people, your God is my God."
>
> —*Ruth 1:16*

Friends Forever
How to be a Good Friend

by Hayley DiMarco

*B*EING A GOOD FRIEND IS REALLY IMPORTANT, not just for your friendships, but for your surrender to God. God wants His children to be good friends.

And a girl after God's own heart is the best friend around, because she loves her friends the way God loves her: with kindness, mercy, and grace. She's there for her friends when they're happy and sad; she doesn't resent their messy lives or talk about them behind their back. She's honest but gentle and generous with her stuff and her time.

Proverbs 17:17 says that "A friend loves at all times, and a brother is born for a difficult time." That means that love is the foundation of all friendship. So, how can you become a better friend—one that truly loves the way God loves? What are the character traits of a God girl with her friends? Here are a few tips that will make you a better—and more godly—friend:

1. **Get over yourself.** Since love is the opposite of selfishness, a true friend is the opposite of self-obsessed. That means she does things that are for the good of others instead of herself. She takes the smallest cupcake and the worst seat. She doesn't argue over boys or the last dress in her size. She isn't looking out for herself, but for others. She loves others so much that she makes them more important than herself, making John 15:13 her standard: "No one has greater love than this, that someone would lay down his life for his friends." That doesn't necessarily mean that to be a good friend, you should take a bullet for someone—but it does mean that you give up your selfishness and put her needs first. It's dying to the urge to satisfy yourself and choosing to focus your life on serving and loving others.

2. **Don't be easily offended.** There's no room for taking offense in friendship. Scripture tells us that love doesn't keep a record of wrongs (1 Cor. 13: 5). True love isn't concerned with protecting yourself or returning insult for insult; instead, it's about dealing with problems and getting over offenses before they have time to fester.

    Jesus is our example in this aspect of friendship. In 1 Peter 2:23, the Bible tells us that when Jesus was reviled, "He did not revile in return" and when He was suffering, "He did not threaten." If anyone had a reason to be insulted by the way He was treated, it was Jesus. But He didn't. If He had all that reason but still didn't take offense, what gives us the right to be offended when people insult us or revile us?

3. **Encourage them.** Your friendships are meant to bring glory to God. What that means on a practical level is that you will choose to be encouraging to your friend and strive to build her up in Christ.

    Your friendships can feed the fire of faith. Godly friends should bring you closer to God and help you grow in your relationship with Him. As a believer, that's also your role as a friend. You should be someone who encourages your friends with godly words and wisdom. Even if your friend isn't a believer, your role is still to steer her to Christ. And that's not just by your example, but also with your words—words of encouragement, not condemnation. Choose to say things that build up your friends in faith

and love. That's the best way to bring glory to God in those relationships. Take 1 Thessalonians 5:11 to heart: "Therefore encourage one another and build each other up as you are already doing."

4. **Love them more than you flatter them.** It can be really easy to lie to your friends in order to make them happy, but part of being a godly friend is being an honest friend. That means that you tell your friends the truth in love, not just what will make them feel good about themselves.

   It also means that the reverse is true: you allow your friends to be honest with you and don't get all upset when they do. When a godly friend corrects you out of love for you and in order to bring you closer to Christ, accept that correction with humility and confession. True friends aren't continually correcting you, but when a godly, loving friend does correct you, pay attention! Remember Proverbs 27:6: "The wounds of a friend are trustworthy, but the kisses of an enemy are excessive." True friends don't correct you to hurt you. They correct you because they love you and want to see you live a life that pleases God.

5. **Offer them grace.** Check out James 5:16: "Therefore, confess your sins to one another and pray for one another, so that you may be healed. The urgent request of a righteous person is very powerful in its effect."

   When you confess a sin to God, He forgives you immediately—but He has also placed people in your life to help you live according to His will. Sometimes, you need someone who knows about your stuff and shows you God's grace in the middle of your mess. You need someone who prays for and with you when you need it. That doesn't mean that you confess your sins to every one of your friends, but it does mean that you have a godly, wise friend who is growing in her relationship with Christ who you can trust to spur you on and still love you when you mess up big time.

You need that kind of friend, but you also need to be that kind of friend. Be the kind of friend who people can be honest with. Encourage your friends to be real about their lives with you and don't respond to their confessions with condemnation. That also means that you can't be loose with your tongue. No talking about what your friend confesses unless he or she gives you permission or it involves something harmful or illegal. If it does, talk with your parents, student minister, or a trusted adult.

6. **Share their joys and sorrows.** Jealousy, envy, greed, or selfishness can all lead you to be upset rather than happy for your friend. But when you get upset because your friend got something that you didn't, you become a mean girl. In Romans 12:15, the Bible tells us to "Rejoice with those who rejoice; weep with those who weep." God wants you to be sensitive to people's emotions and to care about them and their happiness as much as you care about your own.

That doesn't mean that you won't feel jealous, envious, or selfish when your friend gets something you wanted. You will; it's part of our sinful nature. But when you're a God girl, you recognize that those feelings aren't from God, confess them, and ask Him to help you respond in the right way.

WHAT KIND OF A FRIEND ARE YOU?

Take these three mini-quizzes and to find out which friend type best describes you. After each statement, record your answer using the following scale:

0=Not at all   1=Sometimes   2=A lot   3=Most of the time

THE COUNSELOR

1. My friends come to me when they have problems. _____
2. I fit in all kinds of groups. _____
3. I'm a good listener. _____
4. I don't judge people. _____
5. I'm a peace-maker. _____
6. I don't have problems with mean girls. _____
7. I love giving advice. _____

Total: _________

FUN FRIEND

1. My friends would say I make them laugh. _____
2. I get bored listening, I prefer to talk. _____
3. When my friends are bummed, I help them forget their problems by doing something fun. _____
4. I rarely talk about heavy stuff. _____
5. I would rather go hang out and talk with friends than do a Bible study with them. _____
6. I don't take life too seriously. _____
7. I don't like talking about my problems with others. _____

Total: _________

MISS AGREEABLE

1. I like agreeing with my friends. _____
2. I rarely judge people. _____
3. I don't like expressing my own opinions. _____
4. My friends come to me with their frustrations. _____
5. When my friends need me, I am always there for them. _____
6. I'm a good listener. _____
7. I never give advice, only encouragement. _____

Total: _________

Take a look at which quiz you scored the highest on, then read the information below.

THE COUNSELOR: Girls come to you when they don't know what to do, and you like helping them out. But when others share their problems, do you lead them to God's Word? Do you offer them grace and encouragement as well as the truth they need to hear, but don't want to? Avoid judging others and always remember the grace God has shown you. Trust God with your friends' lives; don't try to control them.

THE FUN FRIEND: Your friends feel better just for being with you. But be careful, because sometimes your friends need more than just a good time. They need someone to listen to them, to be real with them, to cry with them, to lovingly hold them accountable, and even to laugh with them. Find out what God considers a good friend and focus on bringing God all the glory.

MISS AGREEABLE: You like it when people like you. Your friends probably love being with you because they know you aren't going to judge them. That's the good news! The danger can come when you become an encourager of sin. Looking the other way when friends want you to encourage or go along with their sin is sin. You can be agreeable and merciful while still refusing to go along with their sin.

THE WORLD HAS A LOT TO SAY ABOUT LOVE.

It's a perennial favorite on the covers of teen magazines, the reason we flock to the theater to see the latest romantic comedy, and the topic of a lot of those late-night text conversations with your best friend.

We love the idea of love—but we live in a culture that's got a pretty skewed idea of what true love actually is. Because true love isn't just that feeling when that special guy holds your hand or the smile you can't wipe off your face when you think about him. It isn't being happy, usually doesn't come at first sight, and is something much deeper than a feeling that can come and go.

WHAT THE WORLD SAYS

A few thoughts from popular culture about love:

- "I've loved another with all my heart and soul; and to me, this has always been enough."
  —Noah Calhoun in *The Notebook*

- ""I'm an-old fashioned romantic. I believe in love and marriage, but not necessarily with the same person."
  —John Travolta

- "Love is a complete mystery."
  —Taylor Swift

Truth is, true love isn't generated by human passion or emotion. Passion and emotion can certainly be a by-product of love, but true love is a result of the Holy Spirit within you. In 1 John 4:8, we're told "God is love."

Love is an attribute of God. It's His very character and nature; it's who He is. And for you to really experience the depths of true love, you have to surrender your heart and life to Him—because when you give your life up for His, you end up with a love only His Holy Spirit can generate.

From God's example, we know that true love involves commitment and—wait for it—sacrifice. Real, true love has more to do with what would be best for the other person than what makes you happy. It isn't selfish and involves letting go of your dreams, desires, needs, and wants so that your beloved's dreams, desires, needs, and wants can come true.

One of the best biblical examples of that kind of sacrificial love is Ruth. Let's take a look!

BEHIND THE STORY: RUTH

Ruth wasn't Jewish. In fact, she was from Moab, a narrow strip of land just to the east of the Dead Sea. The Moabites didn't worship God, instead worshiping a pagan god called Chemosh. According to the Book of Ruth, at some point, Ruth had married a Jewish man who had come to Moab from Judah with his parents, Emilelech and Naomi, during a time of famine. In time, Emilelech and his two sons died, leaving Ruth alone with her mother-in-law and sister-in-law, Orpah. In Ruth 1:6, Naomi began to prepare to return to Judah, having learned the famine was over and food was plentiful. Knowing her daughters-in-law would be considered outsiders, she offered them a way out, telling them to leave her and return to their mother's houses. Orpah went (Ruth 1:14), but Ruth stayed.

On the right, read Ruth's response to Naomi when she questioned why Ruth didn't leave her. Underline all the words or phrases that express Ruth's commitment, sacrifice, or surrender.

But Ruth replied:

Do not persuade me to leave you or go back and not follow you. For wherever you go, I will go, and wherever you live, I will live; your people will be my people, and your God will be my God. Where you die, I will die, and there I will be buried. May Yahweh punish me, and do so severely, if anything but death separates you and me. *—Ruth 1:16-17*

Make sure you understand what Ruth did here. In leaving Moab to go to Bethlehem with Naomi, she was leaving behind everything she'd ever known. Her family. Her friends. The life she thought she'd live. All the familiar places and things she loved. Her gods. Her home. She was giving them all up and going to a place where she knew no one except Naomi.

Ruth was young enough to remarry. Naomi had even told her to do just that (Ruth 1:8-9), but Ruth could not be dissuaded. She insisted on sacrificing everything she knew and taking care of Naomi.

That's true love.

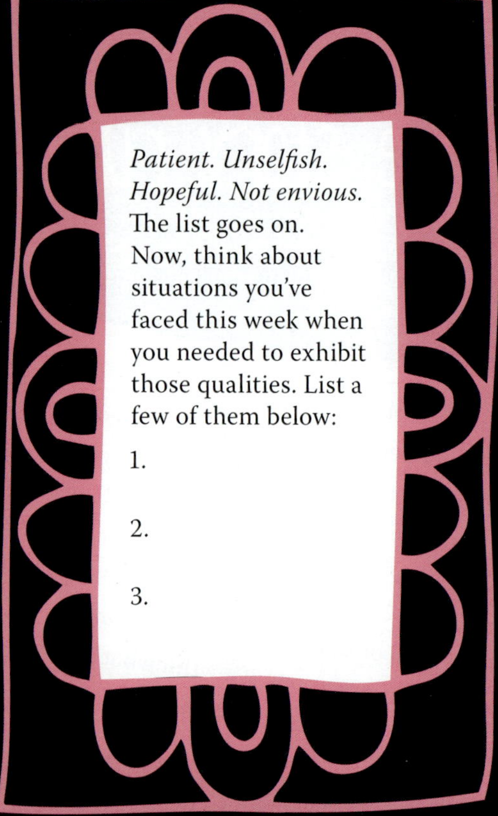

Patient. Unselfish. Hopeful. Not envious. The list goes on. Now, think about situations you've faced this week when you needed to exhibit those qualities. List a few of them below:

1.

2.

3.

THE LOOK OF LOVE

So what are some other examples of true love? Probably one of the most famous sections of Scripture on love (and one that you might have been saving up for your wedding someday) is 1 Corinthians 13:4-7. Check it out below and circle all the words or phrases that describe love.

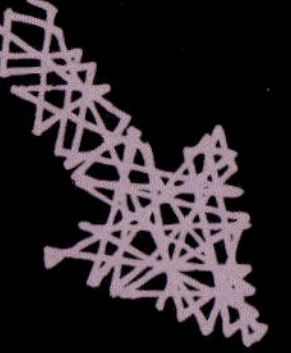

"Love is patient, love is kind. Love does not envy, is not boastful, is not conceited, does not act improperly, is not selfish, is not provoked, and does not keep a record of wrongs. Love finds no joy in unrighteousness but rejoices in the truth. It bears all things, believes all things, hopes all things, endures all things."

—1 Corinthians 13:4–7

The kind of love the Bible talks about has less to do with a warm, fuzzy feeling and more to do with a commitment to put others first. In fact, the opposite of love isn't hate; it's selfishness. Remember that last fight you had with your mom? The one when all you could think about was proving that you were right? When you were distrustful, impatient, testy, and irritable? That was you being selfish—and that's the opposite of love.

Think about your life. In what ways have you failed to love others? Can you remember times when you have put your own feelings before someone else's or when you've been more focused on how you feel than on how others feel? Pray about those times when you've let selfishness have control rather than sacrificial love. Write your prayer in the space below.

Love, True Love

Take a look at each of the following Scriptures. Consider what each one teaches you about real, true love:

- Matthew 5:43-46
- John 13:34-35

Understand this: as one of God's children, love should be as much of your nature as it is God's. And true love isn't apparent in pretty words and feelings; it's shown in your actions. Look to Jesus as your example. What did He teach us about true love?

1. **True love isn't selfish.** If Jesus had been selfish, He would have done what was best for Him—which probably wasn't enduring pain, suffering, and ridicule on our behalf.
2. **True love involves sacrifice and commitment.** It wasn't a warm, fuzzy feeling that compelled Jesus to die on the cross; it was a commitment to us and to His Father's plan to save us. Jesus sacrificed His very life so that we might have eternal life.
3. **True love is characterized by surrender.** Jesus knew the reality of the torture that awaited Him when He prayed "not My will, but Yours" in the Garden. Jesus surrendered His will to the Father's.

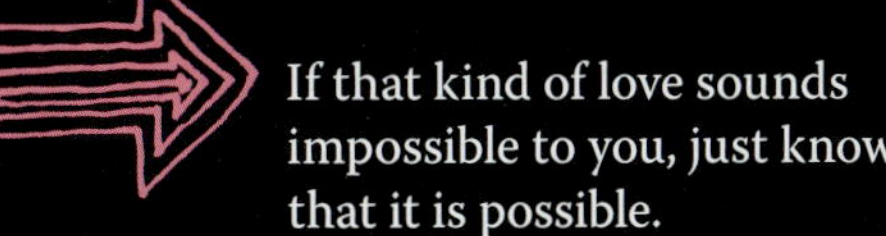

If that kind of love sounds impossible to you, just know that it is possible.

Just look to Jesus.

Remember Ruth.

Recount the stories of people you know whose lives were radically changed by Jesus' sacrificial love.

Set your mind on the things of God, listen to His Word, trust Him, and allow Him to create in you a new heart— one that loves when you get nothing in return, loves when it means sacrificing your own dreams and desires, and loves someone when he or she doesn't deserve it.

IT'S TIME TO SURRENDER TO TRUE LOVE.

Devoted:
A Modern-Day Profile

by Hannah Wakefield

Devoted.

It's a word that means someone is very loving and loyal. And for Elizabeth, the best definition is her best friend, Rachel.

"Rachel always gives selflessly," Elizabeth says.

But that's not all. Elizabeth says that Rachel has often given up her sleep to talk when Elizabeth needed to. Elizabeth clearly remembers one time when she woke Rachel up at 6 a.m., crying. Forgetting her own need for sleep, Rachel comforted Elizabeth and prayed aloud for her friend, through tears of her own.

Rachel's devotion and sacrificial love have been on display throughout the girls' friendship. On bad days, Rachel has taken Elizabeth out for ice cream or left her short notes of encouragement. Once on Elizabeth's birthday, Rachel was a couple of hours away, but she got up early and drove all the way—just to surprise Elizabeth with two dozen doughnuts for breakfast.

That's not to say that the girls' friendship has always been easy. Elizabeth remembers a guy she liked who wasn't very good to her. All Elizabeth saw was that he had the essentials—he was cute, smart, and a Christian.

But he didn't pass Rachel's test.

"I would mention him sometimes, but Rachel never gave in to that," Elizabeth says. "While I thought he was great, she saw things clearly and would point out that he didn't treat people—including me—with kindness."

Just as Naomi tried to push Ruth away, Elizabeth tried to push Rachel away at times. On days when she was stressed out, Elizabeth would shut herself in her room to work and wouldn't reach out to anyone. But Rachel wouldn't accept that. She would still knock on Elizabeth's door, sit on her bed or the floor, and talk. She would call Elizabeth to invite her to things and encourage her to come. In those moments when Elizabeth withdrew, Rachel pursued their friendship.

Rachel and Elizabeth both agree that being a loyal friend doesn't mean you're perfect. They've had disagreements and been selfish and inconsiderate. But Elizabeth says that what makes Rachel a truly loyal friend is that she always considers their friendship important enough to make things right. She apologizes, and she offers and seeks forgiveness.

It's easy to be a friend when you're having fun together, the girls say. But both believe that true friendship happens when you're busy, sick, stressed, scared, angry, or hurting. It involves making hard choices—the choice to not say what you were going to say and to listen to the other person instead, the choice to confess when you are wrong, the choice to pray for another person. It means giving your time, money, resources, and words—your very self—for another person, just as Christ gave Himself for us: "Greater love has no one than this, that someone lays down his life for his friends" (John 15:13).

VOICES

OUT OF HER COMFORT ZONE

"On my first travel softball team I had to try out for, it was the first day of tryouts, and I didn't know many people. My friend came and threw with me when she could've thrown with one of her best friends." —*Grace, 13*

"One time, my friend sacrificed friendship with others just to make sure I wasn't sitting alone." —*Elizabeth, 16*

TIME'S UP

"One night I was really upset because of a boy, and one of my friends sacrificed her night, time, and going out with her boyfriend to come comfort me." —*Alyson, 17*

"This may sound unimportant, but one of my best friends planned a surprise birthday party for me! And once I saw all the planning and decorations and activities we had, I realized how much time she sacrificed and how unselfish she was to make me happy!" —*Olivia, 18*

NO MATTER WHAT

"My friend sacrificed a lot of time and late-night talks to pour into me. She helped me through when my family lost our house to foreclosure, when my dad lost his job, and when my mom was diagnosed with cancer. She has just always been there for me no matter what." —*Kelly, 16*

"Hanging out with me rather than cool people." —*Morgan, 13*

Toxic Friendships: Are You Safe?

by Emily Cole

IT WASN'T EVEN LUNCHTIME, and Ellie had decided this was officially the worst day of her high school career. Her boyfriend of six months told her they needed to take a break from their relationship, she got a D on the math test she thought she'd aced, her history teacher caught her passing a note and gave her detention, and she ripped a big hole in the seat of her brand-new jeans when sliding off the bleachers after a school assembly.

Holding back tears, she met her friend Sarah in the parking lot after school. After telling Sarah what happened, Ellie was beyond hurt when Sarah bragged about making a B+ on the math test. Then, she told Ellie she'd seen Ellie's boyfriend at the movies last weekend with some girl who went to the high school across town. Finally, Sarah looked at Ellie and said she had to go; she had plans with some of her friends. Ellie broke down in tears and longed for a friend who would have reacted differently to her bad news.

Friends can make or break your teen years. (Actually, they can make or break you at any age.) That's why it is so important to choose them wisely. Even Jesus was careful in choosing His friends. In Luke 6:12-16, we see that Jesus spent a night in prayer before selecting the 12 disciples, the men who would one day carry the gospel message. If the Son of God took time to pray about selecting the friends with whom He would spend the next three years, don't you think it's important you take some time to pray about whom your friends should be?

If you've got great friendships with girls who encourage you and support you, be grateful! Proverbs 18:24 says, "A man with many friends may be harmed, but there is a friend who stays closer than a brother." If you haven't yet found that friend who sticks closer than a brother (or a sister), don't worry. Junior high and high school are not the always the best breeding grounds for lifelong friendships. But if the people you hang out with make you miserable and leave you feeling low, then listen up: it may be time to get new friends.

Like Ellie, you may have friends who tend to be unsympathetic when you're having a bad day or think only of themselves. We all know that even in good friendships, we may sometimes hurt our friends. The key is to recognize when a friendship has

moved from the healthy category into the toxic one. Do any of these characteristics sound like they describe a friend of yours? Check the ones that apply.

- ❏ Selfish
- ❏ Unsupportive
- ❏ Competitive with her friends (being competitive in sports probably doesn't count)
- ❏ Self-centered
- ❏ Negative/pessimistic
- ❏ Demanding
- ❏ Inconsiderate
- ❏ Rude to parents/teachers/ authority figures
- ❏ Believer/does not attend church
- ❏ Puts you or your interests down

If a friend of yours possesses some of those characteristics, it is probably time to evaluate whether or not she still needs to be your friend. While it will always be important that you treat her with respect—the way Christ would have—it is not necessary that you allow her unrestricted access to your life. Establishing boundaries can be an important means of salvaging your sanity and perhaps waking up your friend to her destructive tendencies. But if your friend attempts to control you or gets jealous of time you spend away from her or continues with her negative characteristics after you talk to her, these are warning signs that the friendship has grown toxic, and you will probably need to end it all together.

A few tips for ending a toxic friendship:

1. **PRAY.** Ask God for wisdom in how to handle the situation and what to say to your friend.

2. **BE DIRECT.** Have a conversation in person with your friend about why you two no longer need to be friends.

3. **BE FIRM.** Set boundaries and stick to them.

4. **BE PREPARED FOR EMOTIONAL FALLOUT.** Your friend may resort to some unpleasant tactics as she deals with losing you.

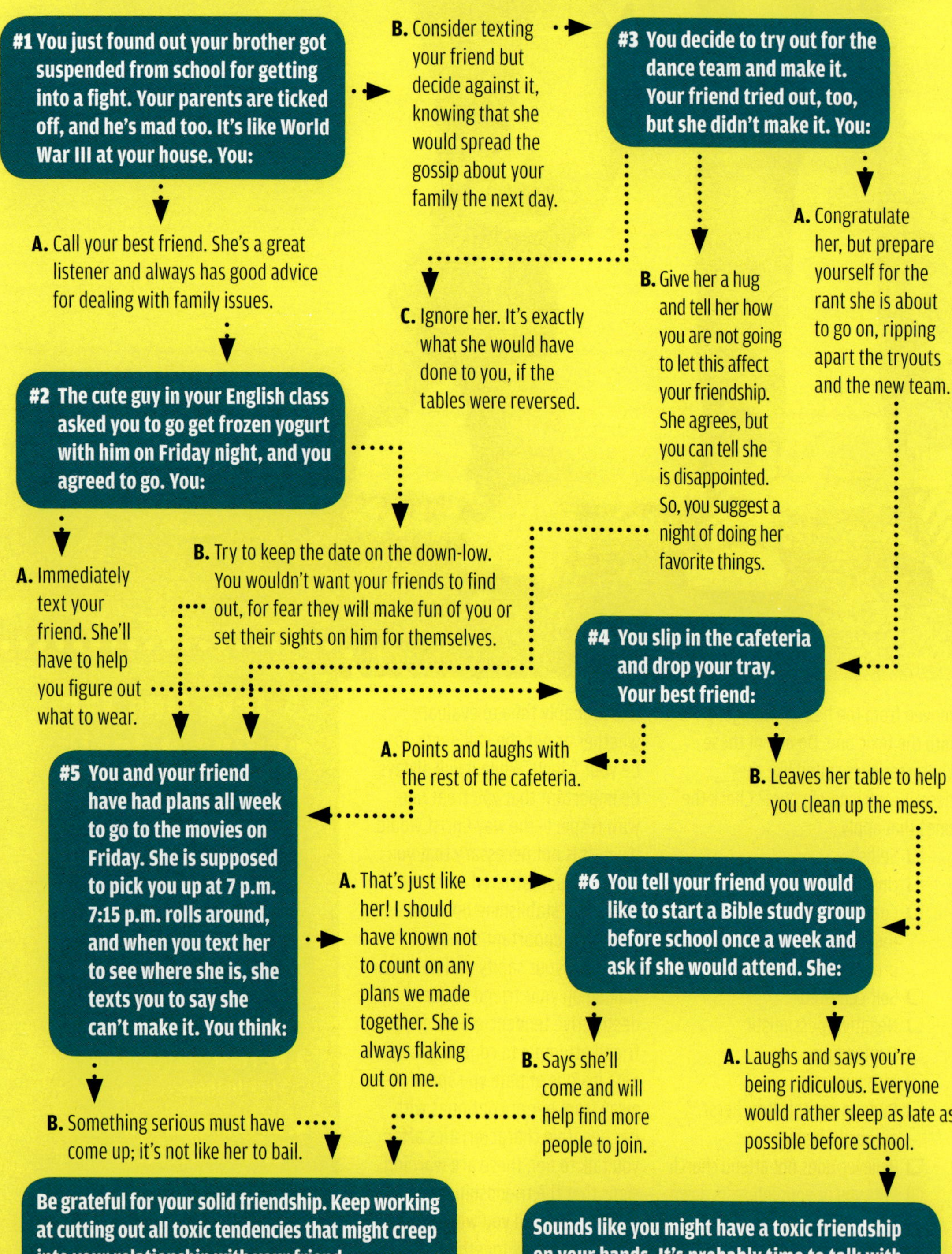

#1 You just found out your brother got suspended from school for getting into a fight. Your parents are ticked off, and he's mad too. It's like World War III at your house. You:

A. Call your best friend. She's a great listener and always has good advice for dealing with family issues.

#2 The cute guy in your English class asked you to go get frozen yogurt with him on Friday night, and you agreed to go. You:

A. Immediately text your friend. She'll have to help you figure out what to wear.

B. Try to keep the date on the down-low. You wouldn't want your friends to find out, for fear they will make fun of you or set their sights on him for themselves.

B. Consider texting your friend but decide against it, knowing that she would spread the gossip about your family the next day.

C. Ignore her. It's exactly what she would have done to you, if the tables were reversed.

#3 You decide to try out for the dance team and make it. Your friend tried out, too, but she didn't make it. You:

A. Congratulate her, but prepare yourself for the rant she is about to go on, ripping apart the tryouts and the new team.

B. Give her a hug and tell her how you are not going to let this affect your friendship. She agrees, but you can tell she is disappointed. So, you suggest a night of doing her favorite things.

#4 You slip in the cafeteria and drop your tray. Your best friend:

A. Points and laughs with the rest of the cafeteria.

B. Leaves her table to help you clean up the mess.

#5 You and your friend have had plans all week to go to the movies on Friday. She is supposed to pick you up at 7 p.m. 7:15 p.m. rolls around, and when you text her to see where she is, she texts you to say she can't make it. You think:

A. That's just like her! I should have known not to count on any plans we made together. She is always flaking out on me.

B. Something serious must have come up; it's not like her to bail.

#6 You tell your friend you would like to start a Bible study group before school once a week and ask if she would attend. She:

A. Laughs and says you're being ridiculous. Everyone would rather sleep as late as possible before school.

B. Says she'll come and will help find more people to join.

Be grateful for your solid friendship. Keep working at cutting out all toxic tendencies that might creep into your relationship with your friend.

Sounds like you might have a toxic friendship on your hands. It's probably time to talk with a parent, trusted church leader, or guidance counselor about moving on from this friendship.

Love isn't about you.

"This is My command: Love one another as I have loved you. No one has greater love than this, that someone would lay down his life for his friends."

–JOHN 15:12-13

{ ASK**HAYLEY** }

IS SHE MY FRIEND OR ENEMY?

Dear Hayley,

My best friend has started being mean to me. It's not all of the time, but sometimes she just blows up at me. The other day she told me that if I didn't let her borrow my favorite pair of jeans she wouldn't be my friend anymore. Help! —*Shelby*

Dear Shelby,

It sounds like you are dealing with a frenemy. Frenemies can sometimes make your life miserable because you never know when they're going to be your friend or your enemy. Take a look at the four signs of frenemies listed below to see if they describe your friend. If so, then it might be time to walk away before she leads you into the sin of resentment, bitterness, or, worse yet, revenge.

You feel worse after being with her. This feeling of discomfort or sadness comes because of her attitude, words, or actions. The feeling might not be overwhelming; it might be just an underlying and nagging feeling that something just isn't right. Sometimes, you just chalk it up to your friend having yet another bad day.

She's overly defensive. Friendship isn't just about feeling good and having fun; friends should make each other better. If you address a sin in your friend's life and she gets overly defensive about it, that's a problem—mostly because she's refusing to listen to God's Word as it applies to her life.

She's jealous. God makes it clear that we need to love one another and not be envious of each other's success. (See 1 John 4:21 and 1 Peter 2:1.) If envy characterizes your friend, she may be more enemy than friend.

She's controlling. When a friend controls you, bosses you around, and manages your life, she's pretending to be God, and you're letting her. A frenemy is a girl who wants to call all the shots. She doesn't trust God with her life or anyone else's, so she controls everything.

THEY JUST DON'T UNDERSTAND!

Dear Hayley,

My parents are impossible. They make me so mad I just want to scream. They don't understand me and think I'm always being disrespectful. They call me a brat! What do I do to make them understand that I am not as bad as they think I am? —*The Bratty Daughter*

Dear Bratty,

Don't freak out! It's normal to have some growing pains—especially since you're now closer to being a grown up than a kid. Understand this: you can't control your parents, but you can control yourself.

Take an honest look at the situation. How do you react to your parents? What do you say? How do you look when you say it? It could be that your attitude and behavior show a lack of respect. Here are some things you might want to quit doing and saying:

- Don't scream "You just don't understand!"
- Don't tell them they are just too old to understand.
- Don't try to hurt yourself to prove to them that you really are feeling what you say you're feeling.
- Don't give them the silent treatment.
- Don't roll your eyes when they are talking to you.
- Minimize your deep sighs when they talk.
- Don't complain about stuff they do, your life, or the home you live in.

Instead, thank your parents often. Speak kindly to and about them. And take the time to pray that both you and your parents would experience more of the fruit of the Spirit in your lives.

HAYLEY DIMARCO is a best-selling and award-winning author of more than 30 books, including *God Girl*, *Mean Girls*, and *Die Young*. Hayley mentors young women online at *GodGirl.com* and runs *Hungry Planet*, a publishing company.

7 ways to love sacrificially this week.

BE QUIET. Give up your right to do all the talking. When you're with others, let them do more of the talking, while you do more listening.

SIBLING RIVALRY. Is there a chore your sibling hates to do? Do it this week with no complaining—or bragging.

THINK ABOUT IT. Memorize Romans 5:8 and ponder Jesus' sacrificial love for you. How will you let that love change you this week?

TAKE NOTICE. Who in your school, youth group, or community is often overlooked? Is there a family member you think doesn't really deserve your love? Do something nice for those people this week, motivated by the truth that God loves them.

YOUR EXAMPLE. Read John 13:1-11. How can you serve others this week rather than doing what's best, easiest, or most comfortable for you?

ENCOUR-A-GRAM. Pick a day this week. Choose to speak words of encouragement rather than negativity at every opportunity.

SECOND PLACE. As you make decisions this week, ask yourself, How can I put myself second? Then, choose to make others' needs more important than your own.

Compelled

In different times and different ways,
our Heavenly Father offers us
a simple proposition: Follow me beyond what
you can control, beyond where your own
strength and competencies can take you."
—Gary Haugen
© GETTY

THE POWER OF PRAYER

by Hayley DiMarco

ONE OF THE GREATEST TOOLS YOU'VE BEEN given as a believer is intercessory prayer. When you intercede for someone in prayer, you simply pray on their behalf. When you pray for your friend who's worried about that exam or that kid in your class who's an avowed atheist, you're interceding for them. Scripture tells us that Esther interceded on behalf of the Jews and saved the Jewish nation. So what can happen when Christians take prayer seriously?

A lot, actually. Let's take a look at a few examples.

PRAYER: TRUSTING GOD

Mary Todd Lincoln, the wife of President Abraham Lincoln, said that after their son Willy died in early 1862, her husband became much closer to God, as is often the case after great loss. In 1863, President Lincoln wrote these amazing words about prayer and our nation: "But we have forgotten God. We have forgotten the gracious hand which preserved us in peace, and multiplied and enriched and strengthened us; and have vainly imagined, in the deceitfulness of our hearts, that all these blessings were produced by some superior wisdom and virtue of our own. Intoxicated with unbroken success, we have become too self-sufficient to feel the necessity of redeeming and preserving grace, too proud to pray to the God that made us! It behooves us, then, to humble ourselves before the offended Power, to confess our national sins, and to pray for clemency and forgiveness."[2] Clearly, Lincoln believed in a prayer that changes not only people, but also nations.

PRAYER: TRUSTING GOD WITH OTHERS

There was once a young man who wanted to be a missionary to Colombia, but he didn't speak Spanish. But that little fact didn't deter him. He moved to a large city in Colombia, rented an apartment, and began fasting and praying for the people of his new country. He prayed for them for 18 years. When he died, he'd hadn't seen one person come to Christ. He'd done no great work other than praying.

A while later, missionaries Lewis and Sally Morely felt God tugging on their hearts for the same people. So, they moved to that same large city in Colombia and opened a small store. They had prepared for the difficult—if not terrifying—job of bringing Christ to a dark land.

But to their surprise, a revival broke out. The Morelys were amazed. How could this have happened? There had been no other missionaries working among the people, no churches, and no revivals. Later, they heard about the man who had faithfully interceded for the people for 18 years and found out that he had lived on the same street as their store. Suddenly, everything became clear. They saw how God had worked through the man's faithful prayers on behalf of the people and had used his faithfulness to plant the seeds of a great revival. You can't say there is no power in prayer.[1]

Hudson Taylor was 19 years old when he realized that God wanted him to move to China and serve as a missionary to the Chinese people. So, he surrendered his life and gave it all to the cause of Christ. But unlike many missionaries, Hudson didn't rely on the church to support his ministry. Instead, Hudson relied on God alone. He was convinced that all he needed to do was ask, and God would supply his needs. He was so convinced of that fact that he told his staff at the China Inland Mission that no one could raise support. Instead, he challenged them to pray for their needs and ask God to support the ministry.

And that's exactly what they did. The staff of the China Inland Mission never went without what they needed. In fact, his organization grew radically. In 1881, he asked God for another 70 missionaries by the end of 1884, and he got 76. In 1886, he prayed for another 100 and got 102. Prayer certainly changes things!

The power of prayer isn't reserved for the super holy or only available to selfless missionaries. It's available to all who surrender their own will to God's. The power of prayer isn't found in the person who speaks the prayer; it's found in the One who answers the prayer. Because of that truth, there's nothing in your life that can't be changed by the power of prayer. There's no disagreement, no pain, no loss, and no disappointment that can't be healed or made whole by prayer.

In fact, prayer is so powerful that if you would only go to God with your concerns and worries, rather than to others, you would see changes in your life that you could never even dream. God can make things happen that seem impossible—and He can change the hearts and lives of people who seem impossible. So rather than trying to change people on your own, trust them to God. Go to the only One who has the power to change hearts and plead with Him for their surrender to His perfect will.

You have been given the power of intercession. Will you use that power or try to change people on your own? Trust God at His Word: "So I say to you, keep asking, and it will be given to you. Keep searching, and you will find. Keep knocking, and the door will be opened to you. For everyone who asks receives, and the one who searches finds, and to the one who knocks, the door will be opened. What father among you, if his son asks for a fish, will give him a snake instead of a fish? Or if he asks for an egg, will give him a scorpion? If you then, who are evil, know how to give good gifts to your children, how much more will the heavenly Father give the Holy Spirit to those who ask Him?" (Luke 11:9–13)

SOURCES

1 From a sermon by Philip Harrelson, "Trading the Superficial for the Substantial" 6/30/08, SermonCentral.com)
2 Source: http://www. greatamericanhistory.net/ lincolnsfaith.htm)

1. HOW OFTEN DO YOU PRAY?

A. I pray once a day at least. *3 points*
B. I pray at least once a week. *2 points*
C. I never pray. *1 point*

2. WHO OR WHAT DO YOU PRAY FOR THE MOST?

A. I have a prayer list of people I pray for. *3 points*
B. I usually just pray for myself and the things I want. *1 point*
C. I start out focused on God and others, but usually end up telling God all about me. *2 points*

3. IS PRAYER SOMETHING YOU'RE PASSIONATE ABOUT?

A. I am interested in learning more about prayer. *2 points*
B. I think prayer is the most powerful tool we have. Who wouldn't be passionate about it? *3 points*
C. I don't think there's that much to learn about prayer. *1 point*

4. DO YOU EVER SEE ANSWERS TO YOUR PRAYERS?

A. I don't think God ever hears me. *1 point*
B. I see a lot of answers to prayer. *3 points*
C. Sometimes. . . *2 points*

5. IS PRAYER A VITAL PART OF YOUR DAILY LIFE?

A. There are a lot of things I do where I can't pray at the same time. *1 point*
B. I pray without ceasing. *3 points*
C. I find myself wanting to pray more and more often. *2 points*

6. DO YOU INTERCEDE FOR OTHERS IN PRAYER?

A. Yes, I love to pray on others' behalf. *3 points*
B. Not really. *1 point*
C. I don't think I know how, but I'd love to learn! *2 points*

WHAT'S YOUR PRAYER PERSONALITY?

Consider the questions about your prayer life below. Circle the answer that's most true for you.

TOTAL: ___________________

16-18 POINTS: Prayer Warrior
Wow, it looks like you have a heart for intercession and love communicating with God. Stay surrendered to God, and your prayers will prove powerful and affective. You do need accountability, though, so find yourself someone who can be your prayer partner (Jas. 5:16).

10-15 POINTS: In Training
You think prayer is powerful and want to learn more about it, even if you don't pray as much as you'd like. Set a specific time each day when you focus completely on communicating with God and studying His Word.

6-9 POINTS: What's the Point?
You can't have a relationship with someone you don't spend any time with. If you want to see what a deeper relationship with God could be like, beg God for more faith, passion, and a deeper desire to get to know Him through prayer. Look for people who need prayer and make them a part of your daily routine. Prayer isn't something you do just when you think you need it; it's something you do because of who God is.

Think about Rosa Parks on a Montgomery, Ala., bus in 1955; Gary Haugen while working in the U.S. Department of Justice in 1997; and William Wilberforce in the British Parliament in 1787. Consider Queen Esther in the Persian court of King Xerxes around 470 B.C.

What do all those people have in common? At a certain place in time, they all faced a moment when each of them said, "This is it. This stops with me. I have to do something about it."

Rosa Parks, tired after a long day at work, refused to give up her seat on a bus and set in motion the Civil Rights movement. Gary Haugen founded the International Justice Mission after working investigations into genocide and oppression. William Wilberforce helped end the slave trade in England, and Esther took a stand for the Jewish people and saved a nation.

Every one of these people did something. See, surrendering to God isn't just a state of mind or an emotion; it involves action. God's love should compel you to take action.

It's also more than that.

Your love should be active because God's is. Take a look at John 3:16 in your Bible or quote it from memory. The point? God so loved the world that He took action on our behalf. God gave His only Son, so that whoever believes in Him should not perish but have eternal life. When we were still sinners, Christ died for us (Rom. 5:8). See, God didn't just talk about loving us; He put His love into action.

And He is our example. God's love is always active—not watching from afar or admiring from a distance, but involved and active in our daily lives. And as you seek to surrender your life to Him, your love should become more and more active.

INTRODUCING ESTHER

Want an example of someone who surrendered her life and was called to action? Need to see God's love in action? Flip over to the Book of Esther in your Bible.

God's name is never once mentioned in the Book of Esther. Even so, the entire book is all about God's relentless, active love for His people, stressing that no matter how much they reject Him, complain about Him, or prove themselves unfaithful, He will always remain faithful and committed to saving them. The fact that God's name isn't mentioned might just be a way of showing how distant the exiled Jews felt from their God as they lived in the land that wasn't their own.

Now for a little background: Esther was a young Jewish girl, an orphan who had been adopted by her cousin and living far from home in Babylon with many other exiled Jews. She was beautiful, according to Esther 2:7, and when King Xerxes found himself in need of a new queen, she was among the many young women taken to the palace for a beauty contest of sorts to find a new queen. Eventually, Esther did become the queen, but chose to keep her birthplace and ethnic background a secret from the king (Est. 2:20).

But Esther soon found herself in a predicament. One of her husband's trusted advisors, Haman, had put a plan to exterminate the Jews into action. He had even gotten the king to sign a decree to that effect. All Jewish people were to be killed. Mordecai, Esther's cousin, alerted her to the disaster that was about to happen and implored her to approach the king and do something to save her people. So, what did Esther do?

Well, at first, she balked, explaining that appearing before the king when he hadn't summoned her was dangerous. The king could even give her the death penalty if she appeared in his court uninvited. But Mordecai wouldn't be deterred. Consider his response to Esther:

"Don't think that you will escape the fate of all the Jews because you are in the king's palace. If you keep silent at this time, liberation and deliverance will come to the Jewish people from another place, but you and your father's house will be destroyed. Who knows, perhaps you have come to your royal position for such a time as this." —Esther 4:13–14

Underline that final sentence from Mordecai's response. Get this: God puts His people in situations where they can act through love, service, and prayer. He placed Esther in a difficult situation and compelled her to do something. Looking back at your own life, can you think of some situations in your past when God has done the same for you? Jot down a few notes about the "such-a-time-as-this" moments God has given you.

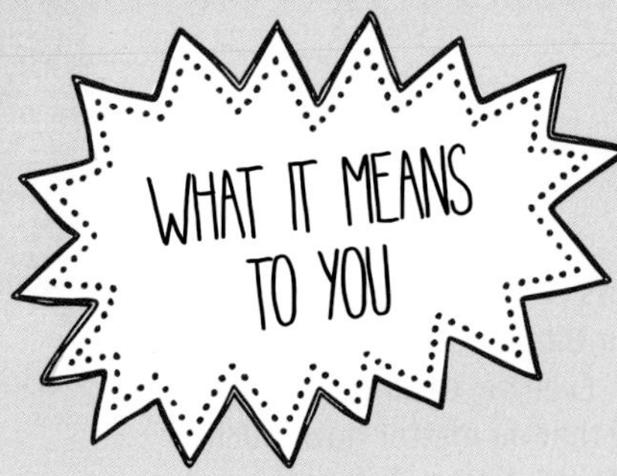

So, what can we learn about surrender and God's call to action from Esther's response? Read over her reply to Mordecai in Esther 4:15-17, then consider the points below.

When God calls you to action . . .

1. You will need support (Est. 4:16). Esther asked that all the Jews fast with her for three days before she approached the king.

2. Seek God and trust Him (Est. 4:16). In the Old Testament, fasting generally implies prayer. The two just go together. So when Esther asked the people to fast, she was inviting them to a focused time of prayer and seeking God. Clearly, she trusted that God could do something about the situation and that prayer was powerful.

3. You will have to risk something (Est. 4:16). Read over verse 16 again. Notice the phrases "I will go" and "If I perish, I perish"? Esther committed to intercede for her people, knowing that it could cost her life.

Esther takes action and pleads her case to the king (Est. 5). Her intercession saved the Jewish nation (Est. 8). The truth is, God wants His people to take an active part in His plan. He wants us to love Him enough that we are compelled to take care of His children, to intercede for them, and help them. Want proof? Check out these verses:

- **Job 42:7-10** (What do these verses teach you about the importance of intercession?)

- **1 Samuel 12:23** (Why would God consider it a sin not to pray for others?)

- **Matthew 22:37–40** (What does it mean to love your neighbor as yourself?)

- **Ephesians 6:18** (What does it mean to intercede for "all the saints"?)

Ephesians 6:18 instructs us to pray without ceasing. When God calls us to action, it will be risky. When we pray without ceasing in those situations, we're showing God that we trust Him to act despite our fear. What risky things do you think God is calling you to do? How will you choose to trust Him with them today? Write your response as a prayer below. Pray it without ceasing!

When you surrender your life to God, it no longer belongs to you (Gal. 2:20). And God wants you to be actively involved in doing His work on this earth. He wants you to pray for others, share His gospel, and help those in need. God is insistent that we be His hands and feet, and that we don't just come to Him with our concerns, but also on behalf of others—those in need, those mired in their own sin, those who are mistreated, abandoned, and oppressed.

You can talk about your love for God and His people, but unless you take action, those are just words. What is God compelling you to do? Intercede for others in prayer? Share the gospel in love? Treat others with respect and love rather than prejudice and scorn?

You were created for such a time as this. Do something!

SKYLER DIDN'T EXPECT TO BE moving to a new school at the beginning of her seventh grade year. And she certainly didn't expect that this move would give her an opportunity to show courage.

The transition was tough. And at first, Skyler found it hard to make friends. But now, a couple of years later, Skyler has a group of friends she loves. Sarah, Madison, Kayla, Sydney, McKenzie, and Shelby really clicked with Skyler. They have sleep-overs, go running together some mornings, and eat lunch together at school.

Simply put, they love having fun.

Skyler is quick to say that these girls are the nicest girls at school. But while the girls accept one another and love being together, they have major differences in their faith. Sarah and McKenzie, for instance, are both atheists. Madison is a Mormon.

Those differences have made for some interesting discussions, Skyler says. Over the years, she's learned how to approach her friends better when it comes to matters of faith.

"I ask lots of questions, and I listen a lot," she says.

Skyler doesn't ever want her friends to feel like she's attacking them. Instead, she strives to make sure they know she really is interested in what they have to say.

But God has also given Skyler plenty of opportunities to share her faith. Sarah's father left her when she was young, and Skyler was able to talk to her about the Father God. Skyler holds on to the hope that the idea of a loving, caring God will stick with Sarah.

Skyler says that Sarah and McKenzie have both asked her how she can believe in something she doesn't see, a question Skyler admits is hard for her to answer. So, she's told them some of the historical evidence for Christ. Ultimately, though, she's explained that it's a matter of faith. If they would just give it a chance and experience it for themselves, they would see, she says.

Skyler doesn't take her responsibility lightly. She believes that God has put her in this position, but also a lot of pressure to not mess it up.

"It's like I've hit a gold mine," she says, "and now I have to get all of the gold."

So what keeps Skyler going while feeling such pressure? Just as Esther's love for her people motivated her to risk her life, Skyler's love for her friends motivates her to speak the truth. Madison is really rooted in her Mormon faith, and Skyler can't stand the thought of not seeing her again after this life. She wants all her friends to be unified in knowing the same God. This is what drives her to share, though it isn't always easy.

Sometimes, Skyler feels like she's not doing much. She's quick to comment that she hasn't seen the results of all the conversations she's been having. But isn't that really what courage is all about?

Courage is about acting in obedience as we trust God to work in his own timing. Esther walked boldly up to the king's throne when she didn't know what would happen, and Skyler continues to share with her friends even though she can't see what God is going to do.

"I know I'm not the perfect messenger," Skyler says. "I make a lot of mistakes."

But Skyler hopes that her conversations with her friends play a small part in God's plan. Now, that's courage.

Esther showed great courage when she took a stand for the Jewish people. When have you had to take a stand?

"When my relationship with a previous boyfriend completely stopped my relationship with God."
—*Nia, 14*

"My friend wanted to have sex with a guy. She tried to convince me it was OK and not a complete sin. I stood up to her and told her what the Bible says in 1 Corinthians 6, that it's a sin—even if it meant losing her as a friend." —*Kelly, 16*

"I had to take a stand when I was at a camp this past summer. My roommates figured out that I was a Christian and viewed me differently for the rest of the week. They were mocking me for all the things I either had or hadn't done because I was a Christian. It was hard at times, but I think they realized that I was serious about my faith and that it wasn't just all talk." —*Haley, 15*

"For a while some of my friends were really into seeing R-rated movies. I don't think that there's anything wrong with it as long as you're the right age, but I usually look up what's going to be in R-rated movies before I go see them. There was a time that this one movie came out and it was supposed to be so funny, but the reviews weren't what I was comfortable with watching and not what I think would be in any way a help to my walk with the Lord. So, I decided not to go, got looked at funny, and stayed home that night. It turned out great that I didn't go because many of my friends didn't like it." —*Alyssa, 17*

FOR SUCH A TIME AS THIS

by Amy Pierson

Live for God.
Do hard things for God.
You need to share your faith more!
All of those things are right but incomplete. The truth is, even on our best day with our best effort, we could only live for God in our own strength for a few minutes.

As Colossians 1:29 reminds us, "labor for this, striving with His strength that works powerfully in me." That means that you should do things with God, not for God. Live knowing that it's His power in you that will make things happen. You are Christ's co-worker, not His employee. He is not far away cheering you on or making demands. He is living inside of you, longing for you to know Him and to allow Him to work in you and through you.

You are in this together!

So what does that mean for your daily life? Let's take a look!

START IN GOD

Spend time reading the Bible to figure out who Jesus is. Pray every chance you get so the Holy Spirit can fashion your heart to look like God's. Remind yourself that you aren't trying to impress Him with your actions. You're starting a friendship with God.

GROW IN GOD

Be faithful to love and trust God more daily. Be obedient daily from the inside out, not the outside in. Esther's decisions showed that she was growing in faith and living in God's power, not her own. How?

Esther obeyed Mordecai even when she was in a terrible circumstance (Est. 2:10). You know as well as I do that obeying isn't easy or natural. We're born selfish, and dying to self and following our parents isn't easy, but it is God's plan. Only God can give you the self-control to not talk back, to be respectful, and to bring joy not shame to your family. Part of growing in God is humbly submitting to authority.

She listened to a wise mentor (Est. 2:15). Sometimes we think we have it all together and that we can change the world for God by ourselves. We have moments that we are completely unteachable, independent, and stubborn. God has placed godly women in your family, church, and community. Seek out women who want to help you get to know God better and learn from them. Part of growing in God's power is depending on others and listening to wisdom.

She was admired by everyone who saw her (Est. 2:15). In high school, there was a very loud and annoying guy in one of my classes. He ate off the floor for attention. He was always arguing with teachers about homework and assignments. Oh, did I mention he was a Christian?

I remember that he was rude and did gross things more than I remember him being a believer. Being different and not caring too much what others think is good. But, being someone who repels—rather than attracts—people to Christianity because you don't care at all about others isn't good. Esther was admired, and she somehow didn't resemble the sin that swirled around her at all. That should be the way you're described, too. Maybe you are so shy no one knows you're a Christian; God wants you to be bolder. Maybe you're like the guy I mentioned above—God wants you to be more kind and understanding. Maybe you need to change your profile picture, because you are causing your Christian brothers to lust and stumble. To love others you must be growing in God.

Grow in God asking Him how you can practice daily obedience and show others that you are growing. Resist discouragement. Remember you are working in God's strength.

GO WITH GOD

When you . . .
- . . . deeply love God, you will naturally love your neighbor.
- . . . truly abide with Him, you will bear fruit.
- . . . spend time with Christ, you will talk about Him.
- . . . work with Him, you will find your purpose.

Esther's a good example of choosing to go with God. She didn't think, *I've been faithful daily. I'm not being rebellious like other girls here. I can totally talk to the king alone.* Esther knew where real power comes from. She called thousands of people to fast and pray for her (Est. 4:16). She knew that going with God—not doing something for God—was the only way everyone would be saved.

I love Esther 4:14: "If you keep silent at this time, liberation and deliverance will come to the Jewish people from another place, but you and your father's house will be destroyed. Who knows, perhaps you have come to your royal position for such a time as this."

Deliverance and relief were going to come from somewhere. God was going to save the Jews with or without Esther. The same is still true. God wants to save, and the rescue will come through someone. Let Jesus shape your heart to look like His— so that your life is shaped by His thoughts, words, actions, and lifestyle. Go with God, like Esther. God wants to deliver and rescue the people of the world—and He wants to use you to do it.

Esther made a decision that changed her kingdom and saved a nation. You can do the same thing. Are you on a drill team with several Muslim girls? Are there some atheists on your debate team? Are you in a student ministry filled with apathy? Do you live in a neighborhood near a retirement community filled with widows you can bless? Are there foreign exchange students in your school or community who don't know Christ? Do your siblings need a kind, godly role model?

God wants to use you in their lives. So, start in God, grow in God, and go with God today!

IT'S TIME TO STAND UP.

"If you keep silent at this time, liberation and deliverance will come to the Jewish people from another place, but you and your father's house will be destroyed. Who knows, perhaps you have come to your royal position for such a time as this." —Esther 4:14

{ ASK **HAYLEY** }

Dear Hayley,

My parents really want me to become a nurse, but I don't think that's what I want to do. I really love to sing, and I want to work in the church, maybe even lead worship someday. How do I convince them that I shouldn't go to nursing school? —*Kaylee*

Dear Kaylee,

Figuring out the future is hard, if not impossible. None of us know what will happen for sure, and we all have dreams—but sometimes those dreams don't come true the way we had imagined. The thing to remember is that God works all things out according to His will, and He uses the experiences of your life to prepare you for the future. You never know, He might want you to become a nurse who sings in the choir and leads worship in children's church. Then, when you graduate nursing school, you can go to the mission field and serve as worship leader/nurse—a double threat!

So, don't freak out just now. Pray and ask Him to give you the chance to worship, volunteer wherever you can, and don't give up the dream as long as God keeps opening doors. But honor your parents as the authority figures God has placed in your life, trusting that He has everything in His sights and will never leave you or forsake you.

Dear Hayley,

Can you give me any advice about prayer? I want to pray, but I have no idea where to even start. Whenever I pray, it's like I'm talking to a wall. How can I even be sure He hears me? Help! —*Chelsea*

Dear Chelsea,

It sounds like you feel like God isn't listening, but that's not the case. He hears you, but sometimes life is so noisy and so full of other voices, you can't hear Him. So, how do you get back on track in your prayer life? Here are a few tips:

- **Worship.** I think the best way to start off prayer is through worship. And that's not just singing songs; it's telling God how amazing He is. Set your mind on God. Think about Him and know that He is thinking about you.
- **Thank.** When you're thankful, it's hard to feel bad. Make a list of everything you are thankful for, even if it's your bed, no homework, or kittens. Add to your list every day.
- **Confess.** The next thing to do is to confess your sin. Agree with God that your sin is sin and ask for His forgiveness.
- **Repent.** After you confess, choose not to live in that kind of sin any more. Express your desire to change and ask God to help you. You need His grace to overcome the power of sin; you cannot do it on your own.
- **Intercede.** If you aren't praying for others, your prayer is weak. It's natural to want to beg God for stuff you really want, but it's important to pray for others.
- **Request.** Even though God knows just what you need, He still wants you to ask Him. Express to Him what you need and want, then tell Him you will be happy with what He provides.

HAYLEY DIMARCO is a best-selling and award-winning author of more than 30 books, including *God Girl*, *Mean Girls*, and *Die Young*. Hayley mentors young women online at *GodGirl.com* and runs *Hungry Planet*, a publishing company.

SEVEN WAYS YOU CAN INTERCEDE THIS WEEK.

1. EYE ON THE WORLD

According to the Joshua Project, there are more than 7,000 unreached people groups in the world. Visit *www.joshuaproject.net* and pray on behalf of a different people group each day this week.

2. OPEN YOUR EYES

Educate yourself about the realities of human trafficking, oppression around the world, and refugees. Intercede for those people in prayer this week.

3. BOLD MOVES

Pray Ephesians 6:19-20 for your Christian friends, asking God that they would be bold to share His gospel to a world that needs to hear it.

4. THE AUTHORITIES

Intercede for your parents, student minister, pastor, and other authority figures God has placed in your life. Share a word of encouragement with them each day this week.

5. COMMUNITY SERVICE

Learn more about the poor, overlooked, and homeless people in your community. Get involved with a ministry that helps them.

6. STAND UP

Have a Christian friend who is struggling with sin? Pray for him or her, but also be willing to boldly intercede and lovingly confront that sin.

7. MORE THAN TALK

Strike up a conversation with the kid at school who doesn't really fit in. Find ways to help others get to know him or her.

committed

"If you do not plan to live the Christian life totally committed to knowing your God and to walking in obedience to Him, then don't begin, for this is what Christianity is all about. It is a change of citizenship, a change of governments, a change of allegiance. If you have no intention of letting Christ rule your life, then forget Christianity; it is not for you."

—Kay Arthur

LIVING A LEGACY

by Hayley DiMarco

When I was in high school, I was . . . kind of a nerd.

I was shy. I had long hair that I would curl, then put into to pigtails high on the sides of my head. I wasn't much of an athlete, and it seemed like everyone at my school played sports.

And to make matters worse, I had decided that I would only wear the color pink. So every day of my freshman year, I wore pink. Needless to say, I was an easy target for the girls who were looking for someone to make fun of.

Unfortunately, the boys didn't see things the same way. The boys really liked me—and I loved flirting. So, I was shy with the girls and friendly with the boys, which led to problems. Most of the girls believed that I thought I was better than everybody else. And that set the stage for the worst four years of my life.

Throughout my four years of high school, the girls did their best to make life miserable for me. One time, I opened my locker and found a carrot carved to look like a person, hanging from a noose. There was a little sign around its neck that said, *Beware of the DOA.* Needless to say, I was freaked when I discovered DOA meant *dead on arrival.* After that, I lived my life always looking around corners, expecting something bad to happen.

Another time, I was hanging out with my boyfriend at his house. He was the quarterback of the football team and a lot of the other girls really liked him, so they decided to get me in trouble. While my boyfriend and I were inside watching TV, the girls showed up and spray-painted nasty stuff about me all over his parents' driveway. Can you imagine?!

The spray paint was permanent, and so was my humiliation.

The pranks went on and on. Over time, I began to harden my heart toward girls in general. I didn't understand them, and I didn't trust them. I feared them. Boys were so much easier to be friends with. They didn't get all catty or talk about you behind your back. By the time I finished college, I had no friends who were girls at all.

I had written them off.

THE REST OF THE STORY

If the story ended there, it would be pretty tragic. But that's not where my story ends. Because one day, I met a boy who told me about Jesus. And that day, everything changed.

The more I got to know Jesus, the more I started to understand His thoughts on suffering and mean girls. As my knowledge grew, I decided to write a couple of books on those topics. So I wrote *Mean Girls* and *Frenemies,* both books where I taught girls how to love others the way Jesus loves us. Through those books, God gave me the opportunity to teach girls across the world how to love their enemies and do good to those who hate them.

And I've been writing ever since.

See, those girls back in high school meant to destroy me. They meant to humiliate and hurt me, but in the end, all they did was help to *make* me. They made me see my need for Jesus. They made me see my sinful nature as a fallen human being. They made me see that I am not alone; there are others out there who suffer—who because of my experience in high school, I can understand and help.

If you had asked me back in high school if I was happy those girls treated me so badly, I would have laughed. Because I wasn't happy they treated me that way. But ask me that question today, and my answer would be a little different. I still don't relish those memories nor do I think what those girls did was right—but I'm also glad they did what they did because without them I wouldn't be the writer I am today.

You may never know the reasons why God allows suffering in your life. The people who have hurt you may never apologize. But when you surrender your heart to God and give Him all that pain, you trust Him to make something beautiful of it. God can redeem the bitterness of your life, so that you can encourage others the same way He has encouraged you.

Understand this: every moment that you surrender to God causes a ripple effect. Every bit of your surrender leaves a legacy. Each moment you surrender to God will change your life—and it just might change the world.

For the follower of Christ, surrender is simple. It's simple because it all rests on something that has already been done: the blood that Jesus shed for you. His blood is enough to redeem every evil scheme against your life and rescue you from every attack, every boring moment, and every tedious task. His blood makes you a child of God. It makes you a part of His story, a part of the way He will bring His love into the lives of those around you.

The truth is, what you do today will change what happens tomorrow. What you think, what you say, and what you do all change the story of your life. So, what kind of story will you live today? If you can surrender your dreams, your family, your fears, doubts, worries—your very life—to Him, your life will become a powerful tool in the hand of the Creator.

And you will live a legacy that will ripple into eternity.

IF YOU'RE READY TO SURRENDER IT ALL, JOIN ME IN THIS PRAYER:

Dear God, I give up. I give up the fight for my life and surrender it all to You. I trust You to take care of me. I trust You to use me. I trust You with everything. Please accept my surrender. Teach me to let go of the things of this world and to see them the way You see them. Teach me to understand Your bigger picture and trust that You work all things together for the good of those who love you. I know that You have worked in me to bring me to this point, and you will work in me even more once I surrender it all to You.

Thank you for Your Son. Thank you for Your love. And thank You for accepting my simple surrender. Give me the strength to do this and follow You every day. Give me Your Spirit to guide and teach me. I will remember You in all that I do and say.

I love You, Lord.

Amen.

WORRIER OR WARRIOR?

Put a check by each of the following statements that would cause you to worry.

I WOULD WORRY IF . . .

1. The news said a tornado was coming through my town today. _______

2. My best friend started hanging out with someone else more than me. _______

3. I had a test on Friday and a birthday party to go to on Thursday. _______

4. My doctor said I had an irregular test result, and they needed to do more testing. _______

5. My parents were gone for two nights, and I had to stay home alone. _______

6. I didn't get accepted to the college of my choice. _______

7. Someone started a rumor about me. _______

8. I didn't have a date for the school dance. _______

9. My dad lost his job. _______

10. My parents had a huge fight and threatened divorce. _______

TOTAL: _______

8-10 points: Queen of the Worriers

You worry 80-100 percent of the time. And that's a problem. As a God girl, worry shouldn't define your life. Scripture tells us not to worry, that God knows what we need and will provide for us. Read Matthew 6:25-34 and memorize verse 34. When worry threatens to overwhelm you, take the time to pray over those worries and ask God to help you trust Him more.

4-6 points: Worry Wart

You worry 40-60 percent of the time. That's better than worrying 100 percent of the time, but it's still not great. Surrender your worries to God. Remember Jesus' words in John 14:27: "Peace I leave with you. My peace I give to you. I do not give to you as the world gives. Your heart must not be troubled or fearful."

1-3 points: Warrior

You worry 10-30 percent of the time. For the most part, you know that God is in control and you can trust Him. Instead of trying to micro-manage every part of your life, your friends' lives, and the lives of everyone you know, you take 1 Peter 5:7 seriously and cast all your cares on Him.

THE TRUTH ABOUT WORRY

There are always things to worry about, but worry doesn't change the things. Worry only changes you from a child who has surrendered to her Father to one who is trying wrench control back from Him. Worry can make you physically sick. Stomachaches, heartache, high blood pressure, headaches, insomnia, ulcers, and skin problems can all stem from anxiety. If you worry 30 percent or more of the time, then worry is controlling your life. Each time you worry, you doubt God's sovereignty and love. Give up your right to worry and see God's hand in your life in everything.

make a commitment: the sweet safety of surrender

by Hayley DiMarco

For many years, I worried all the time. I worried about my grades, my relationships, my future, the weather, food, even clothes. You name it; I worried about it.

Worry and its drama probably aren't unfamiliar to you. What do you worry about the most? List your top 5 worries below.

1.

2.

3.

4.

5.

the truth is, a lot of us, even God girls, struggle with worry and fears. We don't really mean to or even want to, but the worries just keep taking over. You imagine the worst—then you start to panic, agonize, lose sleep, and make choices that you hope will somehow soothe your worried soul.

The problem with that? It's pointless. Muddling through your life with your fears and worries in complete control contradicts the safety God promised you when you surrendered your life to Him. You don't have to live like that anymore.

When I first learned that Jesus would never leave me and our relationship could never be ripped apart, my worry started to become pointless. After all, worry is only necessary for the girl who doesn't have a perfect God who cares for her perfectly. Slowly, I began to learn the safety of surrendering completely to the God who can.

And I found a sweet, safe place of protection and rest where worry became useless.

What about you?

It's pretty clear from the pivotal moments we've studied in their lives that the Hebrew midwives, Abigail, Rahab, Ruth, and Esther, understood the safety of surrendering to God. But what does it mean for you? Let's dig a little deeper into that.

Look up the verses listed in the box and jot down a few notes about what each one teaches you about surrender.

JOHN 16:33

romans 8:28

2 timothy 2:4

romans 8:31–39

So, what does a surrendered life look like? When you're committed to following God, you will . . .

1. Live to please God (2 Tim. 2:4). This verse uses military language to describe our relationship with God. A good soldier surrenders his entire will to his commanding officer. He takes orders and doesn't object, trusting his commanding officer. When your life is surrendered to God, you want to please Him. It's what the Hebrew midwives did when they protected the Israelite babies (Ex. 1: 8-21), and what Abigail did when she humbled herself before David (1 Sam. 25).

2. Trust that God has a plan for good (Rom. 8:28). That doesn't mean that your life will always be free from tragedy, hardship, or problems. But it does mean that you believe—even when you can't see it—that God is working for the good of His plan and His people—for your good. It's what Esther understood when she interceded for her people and what the Hebrew midwives trusted when they chose to respect God's plan more than Pharaoh's.

3. Know that nothing can separate you from God (Rom. 8:37-39). Despite your past or the sins you will commit in the future, you know that because of Christ, God will not abandon you. Rahab must have understood some part of this when she helped the Israelite spies and placed her life in the hands of their God.

4. Understand that life won't necessarily be easy, but you aren't alone (John 16:33). You will face difficulty in following Christ, but you don't have to live in fear, doubt, or worry. Christ has overcome! The Hebrew midwives, Abigail, Rahab, Ruth, and Esther, all faced moments when their fears and doubts almost overwhelmed them, but each woman chose to believe and trust that God would carry them through.

the rest of the story

Surrender doesn't mean that your life always makes sense or even that it will always be safe. But it does mean that in the midst of everything, you know, believe, and stake your life on the fact that God can be trusted. Want proof? Just read the rest of each of these women's stories:

The Hebrew midwives recognized God for who He was and trusted His plan; God rewarded their faith by giving them families (Ex. 1:20-21).

Abigail married David, becoming the wife of the man who soon became the king (1 Sam. 25:39-42).

Rahab left behind her culture and old way of life to live with the Israelites (Josh. 6:22-27). Eventually, she married a Hebrew man named Salmon and her name is listed in the lineage of Jesus (Matt. 1:5). In addition, she's also mentioned in the "hall of faith" in Hebrews 11:31, where she is honored for having the faith to see that God was the God of the whole earth.

Ruth married a man named Boaz, a Jewish man from Bethlehem. You can count King David, Solomon, and Jesus among her descendants (Matt. 1:5).

Esther saved the entire Jewish nation and her actions are still celebrated in the Jewish festival of Purim, which marks Haman's defeat and God's deliverance of the Jews.

These women trusted God and knew the safety of surrendering their lives to Him and His purposes. They were absolutely committed to live according to His purposes. And He used each one of them—in big and small ways—as He wrote His story of redemption.

the ripple effect

The Hebrew midwives, Abigail, Rahab, Ruth, and Esther probably didn't think that we'd still be talking about them hundreds of years after their deaths. They had no idea that the choices they made thousands of years ago would still affect our lives. They simply made the choice to surrender their lives to God—and the ripple effect of that surrender is still touching lives—even yours!

Your surrender could have the same kind of effect. You may never know the difference your life made in someone's life, but you can be sure that when you're surrendered to God, your life is not wasted—and it will have long-lasting effects, even if you can't see them now. God will use your humility, your love, your faith and trust in His sovereignty, your brokenness, and your willingness to do something for His glory. Your simple surrender to God won't insulate you from all trials or testing, but it will guarantee you a life that matters—one that makes a difference.

God can do amazing things when you fully surrender to Him. Just look at the examples of the Hebrew midwives, Abigail, Rahab, Ruth, and Esther. He deserves all of your heart, soul, mind, and strength—your surrender.

Are you committed to Him? It's time to let go.

Write a note to God in the space provided. Tell Him that you're completely committed to following Him, knowing that there is safety in surrendering to Him.

ALMA'S LEGACY: MY STORY

by Hannah Wakefield

THIS IS ALMA'S STORY, but in many ways this story belongs to so many others, including me. Alma couldn't have foreseen it, but her life had a ripple effect, touching more people than could ever be counted.

By the time she was 12 or 13 years old, Alma knew that God was calling her to live a life on mission—and she thought this meant overseas. So she promised God that she would serve him through international missions. But Alma and her family were very poor, and she had to quit school to help provide for the basic needs of her family. She was never able to travel overseas as she longed to do, but God had a different life of mission planned for her.

Alma found her mission in her own household. Her husband, Earl, was a good man, but he didn't know Jesus. So for years, Alma prayed for her husband. Then, when she found out that she was pregnant with her first son, Bob, Alma prayed an extremely bold prayer: "Lord, I will give this child to you, and I want my husband saved."

And with each child following—Bill, Don, and Richard—she prayed the same prayer.

In the meantime, she witnessed to Earl, mostly by asking Earl to come to church with her. And once a year, he would put aside his hunting or his fishing and go to a service with her. When he was about 50 years old, and all his boys were nearly grown, Earl went to a revival service with Alma. That night, the Holy Spirit spoke to Earl, and he gave his life to the Lord.

Alma shouted with joy in the pew as she saw her prayers of many years finally answered.

That was just the beginning of God working powerfully through Alma's family, though. She had given her sons to the Lord, and He took her up on

that. Alma herself couldn't go overseas, but her oldest son, Bob, answered the call to missions and spent his life in places like Malaysia and India sharing Jesus with the people there. Bob's son, Mark, followed in his dad's footsteps, serving as a missionary with his family in the Fiji Islands and is currently serving in Thailand. Today, Mark's two sons are preparing for international missions work, too. Alma's son, Bill, also went overseas to serve as a missionary in the Philippines, and her grandson, Phillip, and his family serve in Indonesia. Alma's son, Don, stayed in Missouri and was a faithful deacon in his church. Don's children are all Christians, also living their lives for Jesus in the States.

And this is where Alma's story touches mine. Alma's baby son, Richard, became a pastor, serving churches in Indiana, Kentucky, Tennessee, and Missouri. Richard's children, all Christians, told his 12 grandchildren about Jesus and taught them to follow Him.

And I'm one of them. Without Alma Wakefield's faith, my life would probably look very, very different.

But my life is only one of many that's connected with hers.

People everywhere—from Missouri to Malaysia and from Tennessee to Indonesia—have heard about Jesus because of my great-grandma Alma. And they have taught others, who have taught others, who have taught others.

Alma's life was simple, but her faith was huge. She simply lived her life surrendered to Christ and His will for her and her family. She prayed for and cared about the people in her own family enough to bring them to Jesus.

And now I can personally testify to the power of a life surrendered completely to God.

VOICES

Esther. The Hebrew midwives. Abigail. Ruth. Rahab. Each of those women surrendered their lives to God and that surrender had far-reaching effects. So who has changed your life, without even knowing it?

"Morgan Evans. She introduced me to God."
—*Kristin, 13*

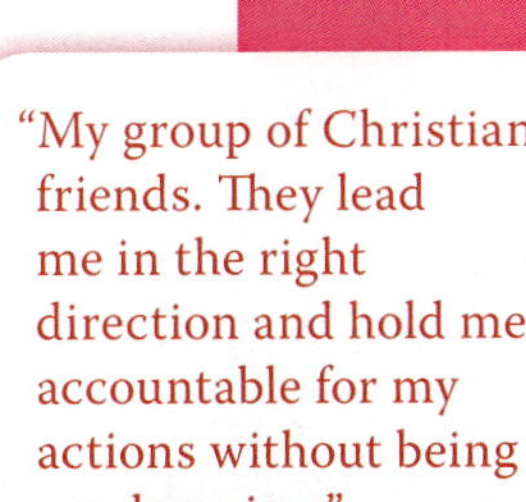

"My old cross-country coach. He was a strong Christian and someone I could talk to and share my thoughts with and always encouraged me positively with good godly advice."
—*Carlyn, 15*

"My group of Christian friends. They lead me in the right direction and hold me accountable for my actions without being condemning."
—*Kayleigh, 14*

"My mom when she had cancer and how strong she was through the whole process."
—*Megan, 16*

"One of my friends lost her dad recently to cancer, and she has trusted in God through it all. I witnessed her deal with adversity in life by completely trusting in Christ. Since then, it has been much easier for me to completely trust in God because I have seen her do it. From all of this, I have learned that it is amazing how much peace you can have when all of your trust is in the Lord." —*Haley, 15*

PART TWO

KYLA'S CHOICE

A "CHOOSE-YOUR-OWN-ADVENTURE" TALE OF ONE GIRL, THE CHOICES SHE COULD MAKE, AND THE RIPPLE EFFECTS OF HER DECISIONS. by Emily White

ENDING A: IF YOU CHOSE TO SEND THE EMAIL, BEGIN READING HERE:

Kyla heard her phone ding, announcing a reply from Gabby. Kyla had been nervous ever since she sent Gabby an invitation to Bible Club. She held her breath as she opened the message:

Kyla,

I was shocked when I got your email! Of all the things you could have been, I totally didn't expect you to be nice to me after everything. I have to admit I'm intrigued. I was expecting you to freak out on me, not invite me to join you! Maybe there is more to you than I gave you credit for. You're the first Christian I've met who acts and talks like she actually believes that "turn-the-other-cheek" stuff. I'm not saying I'm going to join your club, but I'll come check it out. If you really belong to a Bible Club that is as real as you seem to be then I want to know more.

—Gabby

P.S. I'm sorry. I shouldn't have been so mean to you even if we do believe differently.

Kyla exhaled and began to type a reply.

Gabby,

I'd love for you to try things out and meet my friends. Even more than that, I'd love to introduce you to God one day. My friends and I aren't perfect—no one is—but we really do try to live like Christ. The great thing is that when we do mess up, we have forgiveness. That's just one of the many great things about knowing God. I'll see you on Thursday!

Kyla put her phone back in her backpack, unaware that Gabby had almost added one more line to her email. Had Gabby included that sentence, it would have said, If I'm still impressed after spending time at your Bible Club, I might just invite some of my friends next time.

ENDING B: IF YOU CHOSE TO PRESS "DELETE" AND PUT YOUR PHONE AWAY, BEGIN READING HERE.

Kyla was almost to the group of picnic tables. It was the first Bible Club meeting since they had moved to the park. Kyla hoped this would be the best of both worlds: allowing them to avoid a battle, but still showing Gabby that they would stand for what they believe.

Later as Kyla headed to chemistry class, she heard Gabby call her name.

"Kyla, I have to hand it to you. I expected you and your friends to cave under pressure, but you held out longer than I thought you would. I didn't expect you to move your club, I figured you'd just shut down. You're bolder than I first gave you credit for."

Kyla was shocked, "Really? So, does that mean we can call a truce?"

"I think so. Look, I still don't believe in God, but I can respect you for not breaking down or getting all judgmental on me. I don't think we'll hang out together, but I can agree to disagree if you can."

Kyla nodded. "I can do that." She paused, "Gabby? Maybe one day I can show you what we're really about. I'd love for you to get to know God like I know Him."

Gabby studied Kyla. "Maybe," she said slowly. "Don't hold your breath, but maybe one day I'll be intrigued enough to learn more. In the meantime, I'll see you around."

Kyla watched Gabby head down the hallway. She would be praying for future opportunities to show Gabby what true Christianity looked like—and hopefully someday, introduce her to God.

ENDING C: IF YOU CHOSE TO WRITE AN EMAIL INFORMING GABBY THAT YOU ARE STANDING YOUR GROUND, BEGIN READING HERE.

Kyla sighed and reread the email she had sent to Gabby two days ago.

Gabby-

Here is the deal. We don't have to agree on my belief in God or why I think having Bible Club is so important. But, the truth is we have a right to be here just as much as you have the right to protest against us. I hope that one day you will learn why this Bible Club and the God I love is so important to me and why He loves all of us. In the meantime, I hope to show you that He is important enough for me to stand up and keep meeting even in the face of persecution. You can keep harassing us, because we will keep holding Bible Club no matter what you throw at us.

—Kyla

It was Thursday morning—Bible Club morning. After the past couple of months, she had gotten used to heading to Bible Club prepared for a fight, and today would be no different. Kyla scrolled down to read Gabby's response to her email:

Kyla,

So that's the way it's going to be, huh? Fine. I'm impressed with your gutsy move, and I'll give you credit where credit is due. But, don't think this fight is over! You exercise your rights, I'll exercise mine. I'll continue to protest your club; I may even complain to the school board. But, first I'm going to form a Thinking Club—one that will accept and tolerate any religious belief, and we won't try to make people feel guilty about "sin," because we will be accepting of all choices. We'll see who has more members and makes more of an impact by the end of the year!

Kyla put her phone away and turned the corner to head to Bible Club. She would need the prayers and fellowship of her other friends not just this morning, but in the months to come.

KYLA'S STORY, IN A WAY, IS ALSO YOUR STORY. Clearly, the decisions you make can have a huge impact, creating a ripple effect bigger than you could ever imagine. Surrender your life—and every decision—to God and let Him write the story of your life. Then, your story is guaranteed to leave a legacy.

ARE YOU ALL IN?

"Trust in the LORD with all your heart, and do not rely on your own understanding; think about Him in all your ways, and He will guide you on the right paths. Don't consider yourself to be wise; fear the LORD and turn away from evil. This will be healing for your body and strengthening for your bones." —Proverbs 3:5–8

I'M SO SCARED!

Dear Hayley,

My family and I are moving to Kansas, and I am so scared. I am afraid of tornadoes and don't want to live somewhere called Tornado Alley. I don't like the idea of not being safe all the time. I only want to live where there are no natural disasters. I'm so scared. —*Gabby*

Dear Gabby,

I can relate! I hate natural disasters, too; they used to totally freak me out. Worrying over something we can't control is crazy, isn't it? I used to get totally worried when there were tornado warnings until I accepted the sovereignty of God. He's in control. So, now when the siren sounds, I take cover, but I don't worry. I trust Him to do what He does best: take care of things. I pray, and I don't worry about the things I'm praying about— and you don't have to, either. When you surrender your life to God, you surrender your death as well. Surrender to God, so that you can honestly ask that His will be done rather than yours. There's nothing but freedom in that!

OVERWHELMED WITH WORRY

Dear Hayley,

Some girl at school got mad at me and decided to start a nice little rumor about my mom, not me! She has told people my mom is a crackhead. Can you imagine? My mom is so sweet, and I feel so sorry about this, like it was my fault. What do I do? How do I stop these rumors and get this girl to leave me and my mom alone? —*Autumn*

Dear Autumn,

I'm so sorry that other girls use rumors to give themselves pleasure. Trying to control those girls is a losing battle; you just can't. The only person you can control is yourself. So, I suggest that you ignore her. You can't argue with her because there's nothing to argue; her rumors are preposterous. And worrying about how she feels about you or what this will do to you or your mom is like trying to sop up the ocean with a paper towel—it's pointless. Worrying about it only gives the girl the pleasure she was looking for. It's far better to laugh at these situations than to get freaked out over them. Look at this as an opportunity to trust God with your reputation. Pray that God might somehow use this situation to bring this girl into a relationship with Him. Let God change your heart toward this girl and don't let her sin become an excuse for yours. Give up wanting to get revenge or justice, hug your mom, and trust God with the whole thing.

HAYLEY DIMARCO is a best-selling and award-winning author of more than 30 books, including *God Girl*, *Mean Girls*, and *Die Young*. Hayley mentors young women online at *GodGirl.com* and runs *Hungry Planet*, a publishing company.

7 ways you can live a legacy.

#1
Share your story.

Want your life to make a difference for all eternity? Make sharing your faith your way of life. Tell others how God saved you, how He's working in your life right now, and how you can see Him at work in their lives.

#2
Commit to purity.

Remain sexually pure. Don't have sex outside of marriage. Pursue purity in every area of your life, from what you say, think, and do to what you watch on TV or on the Internet.

#3
Meditate on God's Word.

Spend time studying and praying over God's Word. Memorize verses and apply them to your life. Strive to learn what the Bible has to say about how to live your life, then live accordingly.

#4
Become a prayer warrior.

Pray continually, as 1 Thessalonians 5:17 says. Make prayer such a part of your life that you don't make decisions or choose your words without it.

#5
Serve.

Surrender your right to do whatever pleases you in order to serve others. Mow someone's yard, get involved in an inner city ministry, or just listen to someone who needs to talk. Make it a point to put others' needs first.

#6
Be the voice of encouragement.

According to Proverbs 18:21, your tongue has the power of life or death. Choose life. Speak words of encouragement and choose to say things that build others up in Christ, rather than tear them down.

#7
Love.

Make Luke 10:27 the standard for your life. Love God. Love others. Let that love point others to God.

SIMPLY SURRENDER.

"Then Jesus said to His disciples, "If anyone
wants to come with Me, he must deny himself,
take up his cross, and follow Me."
—Matthew 16:24

© GETTY